Make that Grade Irish Company Law Revision

THIRD EDITION

EAVAN MURPHY

GILL & MACMILLAN

Gill & Macmillan Ltd
Hume Avenue, Park West
Dublin 12
with associated companies throughout the world

© Eavan Murphy 1999, 2002, 2006
ISBN–13: 978 07171 4028 2

Index compiled by Helen Litton
Print origination in Ireland by
Carrigboy Typesetting Services, County Cork

*The paper used in this book comes from the wood pulp of
managed forests. For every tree felled, at least one tree
is planted, thereby renewing natural resources.*

CONTENTS

TABLE OF CASES

TABLE OF STATUTES

TABLE OF STATUTORY INSTRUMENTS

SOURCES OF COMPANY LAW

A company is an association of one or more persons formed for a business purpose. There are different types of companies (see chapter 2), the most important of which is the company limited by shares and registered under the Companies Acts 1963–2003.

The main sources of company law are the Companies Acts, EU legislation, caselaw and rules of professional organisations.

Companies Act

Eleven Companies Acts have been enacted, in 1963, 1977, 1982, 1983, 1986, two in 1990, two in 1999, one in 2001 and one in 2003.

- Companies Act 1963 – known as the 'Principal Act'. It is the foundation of modern company law in Ireland and almost all issues are covered in its 400 sections. It is referred to later as CA 1963.
- Companies (Amendment) Act 1977 – simplifies certain activities on the Stock Exchange.
- Companies (Amendment) Act 1982 – inserts certain amendments into the principal act.
- Companies (Amendment) Act 1983 – introduces the modern public limited company. This act also deals with financial issues (see chapters 5, 7 and 8). It is referred to as the C(A)A 1983.
- Companies (Amendment) Act 1986 – deals largely with company accounts and reports.
- Companies (Amendment) Act 1990 – a one issue act which creates the role of the examiner, as explained in chapter 17. It is referred to as C(A)A 1990.
- Companies Act 1990 – this deals largely with personnel of a company: directors, secretaries and auditors (see chapters 11 and 12). It is referred to as CA 1990.
- Companies (Amendment) (No. 1) Act 1999 – a short act dealing with stabilisation matters for securities sales.
- Companies (Amendment) (No. 2) Act 1999 – amended the law on examinerships and removed the statutory audit for small companies. It is referred to as the C(A)(No.2)A 1999.

- Company Law Enforcement Act 2001 – this act establishes the Director of Corporate Enforcement and amended the law on investigations (see chapter 16). It is referred to as the CLEA 2001.
- Companies (Auditing and Accounting) Act 2003 – this act establishes the Irish Auditing and Accounting Supervisory Authority and strengthens the regulation of company auditors. It is referred to as C(A&A)A 2003 (see chapter 12).

Collectively, these acts are cited as the Companies Acts 1963 to 2003 and are construed together as one act.

There are also ninety-two pieces of delegated legislation in force under the various acts.

EU Legislation

The EU Council of Ministers makes directives which must be implemented in each member state. There are many company law directives in force in Ireland as Acts or delegated legislation, eg Part X of the Companies Act 1990 on accounts and audit and the EC (Single Member Private Limited Company) Regulations 1994 (see chapter 13). These directives are part of the EU programme of harmonisation of company law throughout the European Union.

Caselaw

Caselaw or precedent is the system of following similar past cases, eg *Salomon v A Salomon & Co Ltd* (1897) which established that a person who forms a company and the company itself are separate legal entities (see chapter 2). Knowledge of precedent is important in solving problem examination questions.

Rules of Professional Bodies

Professional organisations such as the Stock Exchange and the professional accountancy bodies have internal regulations with which their members must comply.

Company law is classified as civil public law, although there are some criminal elements such as insider dealing (see chapter 8).

The Company Law Review Group

The Company Law Enforcement Act 2001 established the Company Law Review Group (CLRG) on a permanent statutory basis. (Prior to this working groups on company law had produced reports at the request of the Minister for Enterprise Trade and Employment). Under section 68, the CLRG shall monitor, review and advise the Minister on matters concerning:

- the implementation, amendment and consolidation of the Companies Acts
- the introduction of new legislation relating to the operation of companies and commercial practices in Ireland
- the Rules of the Superior Courts and case law judgements insofar as they relate to the Companies Acts
- the approach to issues arising from the State's membership of the EU insofar as they affect the operation of the Companies Acts
- international developments in company law, insofar as they may provide lessons for improved State practice, and
- other related matters, including issues submitted by the Minister to the CLRG for consideration.

The members of the CLRG are appointed by the Minister. The Minister must consult with the CLRG at least every two years to determine a work programme. The CLRG must report to the Minister every year. Its website is www.clrg.org.

2

LEGAL PERSONALITY

Methods of Trading

A company is a legal association formed under the Companies Acts 1963–2003.

A company must be distinguished from other forms of business entities, eg sole traders and partnerships.

A sole trader is simply an individual who sets himself or herself up in business. A sole trader has no separate legal personality, and is liable for any losses made by the business.

A partnership is defined by the Partnership Act 1890 as an association of two or more parties carrying on a business in common with a view to a profit. A partnership is like the coming together of two or more sole traders, where all partners share the profits and losses. Like a sole trader general partnership has no separate legal personality (see chapter 19).

Types of Companies

There are different methods of forming companies, depending on the type of company to be formed.

A company formed under charter is a company which was created under a charter or permission from a British monarch. Such companies are not formed in Ireland today, but some still exist, eg the Royal College of Surgeons.

A company formed under statute is a company which is formed under legislation other than the Companies Acts. Occasionally, legislation may create a company for a national purpose such as Bus Éireann. Such companies are still governed by the Companies Acts.

A company formed by registration under the Companies Acts 1963–2003 is the most common type of company. Registration is the formal process of creating the company according to law. A registered company may be limited or unlimited. A limited company may be limited by shares or by guarantee. A company limited by shares may be a private limited company or a public limited company.

An Unlimited Company

An unlimited company is very similar to a partnership in that the company members are liable for the debts of the company. They may be liable without limit, or the liability of each member may be limited to a certain figure, eg €1,000.

A Company Limited by Guarantee

A company limited by guarantee is a company where the members guarantee to pay its debts up to a certain limit in the event of the company being wound up. Such companies are comparatively rare, and are usually non-profit organisations.

A Company Limited by Shares

A company limited by shares is the most common type of company, where the liability of shareholders for the debts of a company is limited to any amount unpaid on their shares. This type of company is often simply referred to as a limited company, and may be a private or public limited company.

Public and Private Limited Companies

Section 2 of the C(A)A 1983 defines a public limited company as 'a company which is not a private company'.

The requirements of a public limited company are:

1. The memorandum must state that it is a public company, see section 5, C(A)A 1983.
2. The name must end with the words 'public limited company' or 'plc', see section 4, C(A)A 1983.
3. The nominal value of the share capital must be at least €38,100, see section 19, C(A)A 1983.

A company which does not comply with these requirements is a private company. A private company is defined in section 33, CA 1963.

A public company may be created as such, or a private company already in existence may re-register as a public company.

Differences between Private and Public Companies

1. Reason for formation: Private companies are generally formed to take advantage of separate legal personality and limited liability, whereas public limited companies are usually formed to raise

investment from the public. A private company may not invite the public to subscribe for its shares.

2. There is no minimum nominal value for the authorised share capital in a private company, whereas a public limited company must have a minimum nominal value of €38,100.

3. A private company needs only a certificate of incorporation to commence trading, whereas a public limited company, if formed as such, must also obtain a certificate to commence trading.

4. There must be some restriction on the transfer of shares in a private company. In a public limited company shares are freely transferable.

5. Since the EC (Single Member Private Company) Regulations 1994, a private company can have one shareholder. The maximum number is 50 since the CA 1963. A public company must have at least seven shareholders, see section 5, CA 1963.

6. Small and medium sized private companies are exempt from some of the provisions of the Companies (Amendment) Act 1986 in relation to the provision of financial information. The Companies (Amendment) (No. 2) Act 1999 removed the statutory audit for small private companies.

7. A private company may have a 'director for life' under section 182, CA 1963 (see chapter 11).

8. The name of the company will reflect whether a company is private or public, as will the memorandum of association.

Listed and Unlisted Companies.

A listed company is a public company the shares of which are bought and sold on the Stock Exchange. Only a small percentage of plcs are listed companies, the others are referred to as unlisted companies.

Group Companies

In a group of companies, a holding company will hold shares in a number of subsidiaries. A company may wish to separate its areas of business for management and administration reasons.

Under section 155 of the CA 1963, a company is a subsidiary of another if that other:

1. is a member of the company and controls the composition of the board of directors, or

2. holds more than half the nominal value of its equity share capital, or

3. holds more than half the nominal value of its shares carrying voting rights (other than voting rights which arise only in specified circumstances), or
4. the first mentioned company is a subsidiary of any company which is the other's subsidiary.

Features of a Company

1. Separate Legal Personality

The company becomes a legal person in its own right, distinct from the share holders and management. Separate legal personality allows this artificial legal person to make contracts, employ people, borrow and pay money, sue and be sued in its corporate name etc as a person would.

Saloman v A Salomon & Co Ltd (1897)
Held: Mr Salomon was a separate legal personality from the defendant company which he formed and was the major shareholder in that company.

2. Limited Liability

Limited liability results from separate legal personality. The liability of the shareholders of a company for the company's debts is limited to any money they owe for their shares.

3. Perpetual Succession

Once a company is formed perpetual succession ensures it will continue until it is wound up. The death of some or all of the shareholders has no effect on the legal existence of the company.

4. Transferability of Shares

Shares in a public limited company are freely transferable. Shares in a private limited company may be transferred subject to some restrictions (see chapter 6).

5. Assets and Liabilities Belong to the Company

All the assets and liabilities of a company belong to the company as a separate legal personality, not to the shareholders or management.

Macaura v Northern Assurance Co Ltd (1925)
Macaura incorporated his forestry business as a company. Some
months later, the forest was destroyed by fire and it was discovered
that the insurance was still in Macaura's name.
Held: The insurance claim failed because the forest belonged to the
company and was uninsured by the company.

7. Capital Maintenance

Companies are subject to strict rules on maintaining the capital
invested in the company (see chapter 7).

8. Ownership and Management

Companies are owned by the shareholders, but managed by the directors. In some companies these positions are held by the same people.

9. Regulation

Companies are regulated externally by the Companies Acts 1963–
2003 and EC legislation, and internally by their own memorandum
and articles of association.

(Note: The above list can also be regarded as a list of the advantages
of trading as a company.)

The disadvantages of trading as a company are:

1. The cost of incorporating and administering a company may be a
   deterrent to a very small business.
2. The Companies Acts have made the regulation of a small company unnecessarily complex, so some businesses may prefer to
   stay as sole traders or partnerships.
3. A company must make certain information available to the public.
   (However, allowances are made for a small private company
   in relation to what it needs to disclose, notably removal of the statutory audit for small private limited companies by the Companies
   (Amendment) (No. 2) Act 1999 (see chapter 3).

Corporate Personality

The key feature of a company is that it is separate in law from its
shareholders, ie it is a separate legal person. This separation is known
as the corporate veil.

Salomon v A Salomon & Co Ltd (1897)
Mr Salomon incorporated his business, selling it for 99 per cent of the shares and a debenture of €12,700. A Salomon & Co Ltd went into insolvent liquidation.
Held: Mr Salomon as a secured debenture holder was separate from A Salomon & Co Ltd, which he had formed. A Salomon & Co Ltd had to repay Mr Salomon first as a secured creditor.

Macaura v Northern Assurance Ltd (1925)
The separate corporate personality of the company and its main shareholder-director meant that the company's main asset was uninsured.

Lee v Lee's Air Farming Ltd (1962)
Held: Mr Lee as an employee was separate from Lee's Air Farming, the company which he had formed and run.

Battle v Irish Art Promotion Centre Ltd (1968) Ire.
The plaintiff who was the major shareholder and Managing Director of Irish Art Promotion Centre Ltd sought to represent the company in court.
Held: As a consequence of a company's separate legal personality only counsel or a solicitor may address the court. The plaintiff was therefore unable to do so.

Lifting the Corporate Veil

The corporate veil can be lifted in two ways, by specific provision in legislation and by discretion of the courts. The three main reasons why this may be done are:

1. to enforce the provisions of company law (when legislation lifts the corporate veil, it is mainly for this reason)
2. to avoid fraud (the most commonly used category by the courts)
3. to deal with a group of companies.

1. Lifting the Veil by Legislation (takes place automatically)

(a) Minimum Membership

Section 36, CA 1963: A shareholder who knows that the company is carrying on business with less than the statutory minimum membership, for more than six months, is severally liable for the debts of the company contracted during that time.

(b) Failure to Use Proper Name

Section 114, CA 1963: If a company fails to affix its name properly on its place of business, letters, documents, cheques or bills of exchange, the company and officers will be liable to a fine.

Durham Fancy Goods v Michael Jackson (Fancy Goods) Ltd (1968)
The defendants endorsed a cheque made out to 'M Jackson (Fancy Goods) Ltd'.
Held: The plaintiffs had accepted an incorrect version of the name, and therefore could not rely on section 114.

Lindholst & Co A/S v Fowler (1988)
The defendant was a director of the Corby Chicken Co Ltd. The defendant signed cheques referring to the 'Corby Chicken Co'.
Held: The defendant was liable under section 114.

(c) No Certificate to Commence Trading as a Public Limited Company

Section 6, C(A)A 1983: The officers of a newly incorporated plc which trades without a certificate to commence trading will be liable to a fine.

(d) Fraudulent Trading

Section 297, CA 1963 (as inserted by section 138, CA 1990): Any person knowingly a party to fraudulent trading may be personally liable without limit for the debts of the company (see chapter 18).

(e) Reckless Trading

Section 297, CA 1963 (as inserted by section 138, CA 1990): Any officer knowingly a party to reckless trading may be personally liable without limit for the debts of the company (see chapter 18).

(f) Taxation

Legislation dealing with Income Tax, Corporation Tax and Capital Gains Tax contains many instances where the corporate veil may be lifted to treat companies and their owners together.

2. Lifting the Veil by the Courts (this is discretionary)

(a) The Company was Formed for Fraudulent Purposes
Gilford Motor Co v Horne (1933)
Held: A company set up to avoid an employment restraint of trade clause was formed for an improper purpose and the veil of incorporation was lifted.

Jones v Lipman (1962)
L contracted to sell his house to J, but then formed a company and conveyed the house to it to prevent the sale.
Held: The company was a 'device or sham' formed for an improper purpose. The corporate veil was lifted and the house was sold to J as agreed.

Roundabout Ltd v Beirne (1959) Ire.
Held: A company set up to break a trade dispute was 'a legal subterfuge' but a legitimate one.

(b) Group Companies

The courts will lift the veil in cases of group companies if to do so reflects the economic and commercial realities of the situation.

Power Supermarket v Crumlin Investments and Dunnes Stores (Crumlin) Ltd (1981) Ire.
In a dispute over restrictive trading covenants in supermarket leases, it emerged that each Dunnes Stores shop traded as a separate company, controlled by the same people.
Held: The court lifted the corporate veil to consider the reality of the Dunnes Stores group of companies, because 'the justice of the case so requires it'.

State (McInerney & Co Ltd) v Dublin County Council (1985) Ire.
Held: A subsidiary company could not to seek to raise the corporate veil by arguing that it was part of the holding company, as 'the corporate veil is not a device to be raised or lowered at the option of the parent company or group. The arm which lifts the corporate veil must be that of equity'.

Lac Minerals Ltd v Chevron Minerals Corporation of Ireland Ltd and others (1995) Ire.
Held: Where it is sought to lift the corporate veil in relation to a group of companies, two requirements must be satisfied:

(i) the acts of one company must be factually identified with another company, and
(ii) there must be circumstances where justice would be served only if the court ignores the distinction of the separate companies.

3. If the Court is Exercising a Discretion (this is a catch-all category)

Re Bugle Press Ltd (1961)
Held: A company set up to take over another company against the will of a minority shareholder was formed for an improper purpose.

Re Murph's Restaurant Ltd (1979) Ire.
Two shareholder-directors removed the third from the company after their personal relationships soured. In response, the third man sought to wind up the company under section 213(f), CA 1963 on the grounds of oppression as provided for in section 205, CA 1963.
Held: It was just and equitable to lift the corporate veil and wind up the company, because the removal of the third man damaged a relationship based on 'mutual trust and confidence' which was more akin to a partnership than a company.

Reynolds v Malocco trading as 'Patrick' (1998) Ire.
The plaintiff sought an injunction to prevent publication of a defamatory magazine article. The courts considered the likelihood of his recovering damages from a newly formed company with a €2.5 share capital, by lifting the corporate veil and looking at the reality of the situation.

The decisions in *McInerney's* and *Lac Minerals* can also be seen as examples of the court exercising its discretion based on the justice of the case.

3

FORMATION OF A COMPANY

Incorporation

To incorporate a company, documents must be prepared and lodged with a fee in the Companies Registration Office in Parnell Square Dublin. Where a public company is being formed, the initial sale of shares to the public, the 'flotation', will be done through an issuing house and will be subject to detailed scrutiny and regulation. The person who forms the company is know as the 'promoter'.

Promoter

A company promoter as defined in *Twycross v Grant* (1877) is 'one who undertakes to form a company with reference to a given project and to set it going, and who takes the necessary steps to accomplish that purpose'. The promoter is usually the person who decides to set up the business.

Promoters must use due skill and care in the performance of their duties, and owe fiduciary duties to the company they are forming (ie a duty to act in the best interest of another.) The promoter's duties cover the avoidance of a conflict of interest and the making of full disclosure of profit or interest. A typical nineteenth-century fraud by a promoter was the sale of his own property to the newly formed company at a large, undisclosed profit without disclosure of ownership. If a promoter was found to be in breach of his duty to a company, the contract for the sale of property could be rescinded and damages recovered. This problem rarely arises with modern companies.

Pre-incorporation Contracts

Section 37, CA 1963: A company may adopt or ratify a pre-incorporation contract made on its behalf after it has been incorporated. However, the company is not bound to ratify such a contract, and in such a case the promoter is personally liable on the contract. To cover the possibility that the company might not ratify the contract, the promoter will usually seek to exclude personal liability for any contracts she/he made on behalf of the company. As this is obviously unsatisfactory to the party contracting with the promoter, very few pre-incorporation contracts are made in practice.

Registration Documentation

The promoter prepares the documentation and presents it to the Registrar of Companies, along with the appropriate fee. If everything is in order, the Registrar issues a Certificate of Incorporation. A Certificate to Commence Trading for a plc will be issued by the Minister shortly after incorporation. The incorporation is advertised in Iris Oifigiúil.

Documents for Registration

The documents which must be registered are:

1. The Memorandum of Association
2. The Articles of Association
3. Form A1. The form A1 is a form which contains details of:

  - particulars of the first directors and secretary (who must also sign the form)
  - the address of the company's registered office
  - a statutory declaration by a solicitor engaged in the formation of the company or by a person named as director or secretary that the registration requirements of the Companies Acts 1963–2003 have been complied with
  - a statement of capital, detailing the classes of shares, nominal value and number of shares authorised and issued. If the company is a public limited company it must register with a minimum authorised share capital of €38,100.

A fee must be paid on registration.

If the registration documents are in order, a Certificate of Incorporation will be issued and also a Certificate to Commence Trading in the case of a plc.

The Certificate of Incorporation proves:

- that the company has been registered and upon what date
- whether it is a private or public company
- that the requirements of the Companies Acts 1963–2003 have been complied with.

A Certificate to Commence Trading in a plc, under section 6, C(A)A 1983 states:

- that the nominal value of allotted shares is not less than €38,100
- the amount of paid up allotted capital (which must be at least 25 per cent of the nominal value of allotted shares)
- details of any preliminary expenses
- details of any benefits to a promoter.

It is an offence to trade without a Certificate to Commence Trading, but any contracts made by the company are still valid. The corporate veil may be lifted and a company may be struck off the register for failure to get such a certificate, as explained in the last chapter.

Re-registration

It is possible for a private company to re-register and thereby change its status from a private company to a plc. A special resolution must be passed and an application made to the Registrar of Companies. Additionally,

- the share capital must be at least €38,100 with one quarter paid up
- net assets must be at least equal to the total of the called up share capital and undistributable reserves.

Such re-registration is common and no certificate to commence trading is required.

To re-register as a public company, the private company must pass a special resolution to alter its articles of association to add the four restrictions on a private company in section 33, CA 1963 (see above).

It is also possible, but less common, for a public company to re-register as a private company. A limited company may re-register as an unlimited company with the consent of all the shareholders.

Registered Office

Every company must have a registered office for keeping statutory registers and the delivery of official documents.

Companies Registration Office

The Companies Registration Office is the central state office dealing with practical aspects of company law, such as the incorporation of new companies and the filing of the annual return. It is run by the Registrar of Companies under the Department of Enterprise, Trade and Employment, and is located in Parnell Square Dublin. The registration and other documents which a company is obliged to file are open to inspection by the public on payment of a small fee. The Companies Registration Office website is at www.cro.ie.

Company Records

The following company records must be kept at the registered office of a company:

1. the register of members, under section 116, CA 1963
2. the register of debenture holders, under section 91, CA 1963
3. the register of directors and secretaries, under section 195, CA 1963
4. the register of directors' and secretaries' interests in shares, under section 59, CA 1990
5. the register of interests in shares in public companies, under section 80, CA 1990
6. a directors' conflict of interest book, under section 194, CA 1963
7. copies of instruments creating charges, under section 109, CA 1963
8. the books containing minutes of general meetings and directors meetings, under section 145, CA 1963
9. the books of account, under section 202, CA 1990.

Company Accounts

A company is obliged to maintain a number of basic account records. These are:

1. Books of account (or primary records). According to section 202, CA 1990 (replacing section 147, CA 1963), every company must keep 'proper books of account' of company transactions, which are available to company officers only. These accounts must comply with the requirements of legislation and give a true and fair view of the company's financial situation.

2. Balance sheet and profit and loss account. These are available to company shareholders at general meeting. Under section 149, CA 1963, the accounts must comply with legislation and give a true and fair view of the profit or loss of the company for the financial year.

3. Accounts to be filed in Companies Registration Office, (the 'annual return'). Small and medium sized companies, based on certain features, are given concessions in relation to what has to be published under the 1986 Act. The Company Law Enforcement Act 2001 provides sanctions for failure to comply with filing obligations.

Small Private Company

A small private company is one which satisfies two of three conditions:

- a balance sheet total of less than €1.9 million
- turnover of less than €3.81 million
- average number of employees less than 50.

A small private company does not file a profit and loss account and files an abridged balance sheet and certain notes to the accounts.

Medium Sized Company

A medium sized company must satisfy two of three conditions:

- a balance sheet total of less than €7.6 million
- turnover of less than €15.24 million
- average number of employees less than 250.

A medium sized company files a profit and loss account which begins at gross profit, ie they need not disclose turnover and cost of sales.

Large Private Company

A large private company is any company which does not come within the above two categories. A large company is not given any concessions from publication.

Removal of Statutory Audit

Sections 31–39 of the Companies (Amendment) (No. 2) Act 1999, as amended by section 53 Companies (Auditing and Accounting) Act 2003, removes the requirement for a statutory audit for certain private limited companies. In a suitable company where:

- the turnover does not exceed €1.5 million
- the balance sheet total does not exceed €1.9 million
- the average number of employees does not exceed 50
- it is not a subsidiary, a bank or an insurance company

the directors can decide to avail of the exemption from having accounts audited. (Thus section 160, CA 1963 will not apply, and a company may remove its auditor (see chapter 12).) A shareholder with ten per cent of the votes may prevent a company from availing of the exemption in a given year.

Publication of Company Information

The following information about a company is available:

1. The company's file at the Companies Registration Office in Parnell Square, which can be accessed by the public.
2. The company's statutory registers and books which must be kept at the company's registered office. Some of these are available to the public, and some are only available to company shareholders.
3. Iris Oifigiúil (an official government publication) – certain notices, such as the incorporation or liquidation of a company must be published in Iris Oifigiúil and/or a daily newspaper.
4. The letterheads and documents of a company give basic information about the directors, the registered number of the company and the address of its offices.

4

MEMORANDUM OF ASSOCIATION

Memorandum and Articles of Association

Every company must have a memorandum and articles of association. Under section 80, CLEA 2001 the Registrar may accept documents for registration containing standard form text from the objects clause of a memorandum or articles of association. According to section 6, CA 1963, the memorandum must contain:

1. the company's name
2. its objects
3. a limited liability clause which simply states that 'the liability of the members is limited'
4. a capital clause which states the amount of the nominal capital, the number, division and amount of each share, and
5. an association clause which gives the name, address and occupation of each subscriber, along with the number of shares taken.

The memorandum is also signed by the first subscriber or subscribers, names the first directors and gives the location of the company's registered office.

The Name Clause

Section 6, CA 1963 declares that the company name must end with 'limited' or 'public limited company', unless the Registrar of Companies grants an exemption to a non-profit company such as a charity. It is an offence for anybody other than a plc to trade under a name which ends in plc.

Undesirable Names

Under section 21, CA 1963, the Registrar of Companies may refuse to register a company with an undesirable name, such as:

- an offensive or blasphemous name
- one which implies state sponsorship

- the words 'bank', 'society' or 'insurance' in its name, without permission
- one which is the same or similar to an existing company's name or trademark.

Under section 23, CA 1963, the Registrar of Companies may order a company to change its name within six months of incorporation if its name is too similar to one which has already been registered. An action in passing off can be taken against a new company name which causes confusion with an existing company. Damages are payable.

Ewing v Buttercup Margarine Co Ltd (1917)
Held: The Buttercup Dairy Co got an injunction to prevent a new company operating as the Buttercup Margarine Co Ltd, as there could be confusion between the two businesses.

Muckross Park Hotel Ltd v Randles (1995) Ire.
The plaintiff operated the 'Muckross Park Hotel', which was a Grade A hotel. Another Grade A hotel called the 'Muckross Court Hotel' opened nearby. The plaintiff sought an injunction to stop the defendants using the word 'Muckross' in their name.
Held: This was a case of passing off, where the defendants had infringed the goodwill of the plaintiffs. An injunction was granted to restrain the defendants from using that name.

Guinness Ltd, Smithwick and Sons of Kilkenny v Kilkenny Brewing Company Ltd (1999) Ire.
Held: The defendants were ordered to change their company name because of the likelihood of confusion with 'Kilkenny Irish Beer', which is brewed by the plaintiffs. The plaintiffs had established good will in the word 'Kilkenny' when used in conjunction with 'beer'.

Changing a Company Name

A company may change its name by special resolution passed by 75 per cent of the shareholders, and the Registrar of Companies must also consent to the new name.

Display of a Company Name

Section 114, CA 1963 states that a company must display its name at its office or place of business, on all business letters and notices, cheques, invoices and receipts. Failure to do so may lead to the lifting of the corporate veil (see *Durham Fancy Goods v Michael Jackson (Fancy Goods) Ltd* and *Lindholst & Co A/S v Fowler* in chapter 2).

Company Seal

A company must have a company seal engraved with its name in legible characters.

Registration of Business Names

Any business, including a company, may trade under a business name other than its own name, provided the business name is registered under the Registration of Business Names Act 1963. This business name must be stated on all documents and displayed in the registered office. Registration of a business name under this act does not protect it from duplication, nor does it imply that the name will subsequently be accepted as a company name.

Domain Names

An emerging issue relevant to company names is Internet domain names. The registration of domain names under the top-level domain IE is administered by the IE Domain Registry at www.domainregistry.ie. A company may register an IE domain name provided it is derived from the full legal name of the company, subject to certain rules. Words such as 'limited' and 'plc' may be omitted from the domain name. A company may also register a registered business name as a domain name. The registry will seek proof of the company's legal status and its connection to Ireland.

The Objects Clause

The objects of a company are the company aims, ie what it was set up to do. A company can have any legal activity as one of its objects. A company is not permitted to go beyond its objects by virtue of the ultra vires rule.

A company will also have powers, which are ways of achieving the objects. Most companies have similar powers, eg to buy and sell, hire and fire, write cheques and borrow money. A company will have expressed and implied powers. Implied powers enable a company to do what is normal in the circumstances. A company's powers can only be used to achieve its objects.

Re German Date Coffee Co (1882)

Making coffee from dates was the company's main object, but it began to make coffee from coffee beans instead.
Held: The company could only use its powers to make coffee from dates, so the company had exceeded its powers. (The making of the coffee from coffee beans was also ultra vires.)

Introductions Ltd v National Provincial Bank (1970)
Held: A company used its power to borrow for a purpose which was outside its objects. The borrowing was *ultra vires*.

Companies often use very wide 'independent objects clauses' where all objects are said to be independent of each other. There are also 'Bell House' clauses which allow companies to carry on any business which the directors believe would be advantageous to the company (from *Bell Houses Ltd v City Wall Properties Ltd* (1966))

The Ultra Vires Rule

If a company does something outside the scope of its objects, it is known as ultra vires or 'beyond the powers' of the company. Any such contracts are void. (In practice, to avoid the ultra vires rule, companies are registered with very long lists of objects.)

1. The Pre-1963 Position

A third party who dealt with a company had constructive knowledge of its objects, which were public information through registration. This led to unfairness:

Re Jon Beauforte (1953)
A company changed from making costumes to wood panelling. Subsequently the company ordered fuel for the new business.
Held: This was ultra vires and the fuel supplier could not recover payment for the fuel because he had constructive knowledge that the contract was ultra vires.

Introductions Ltd v National Provincial Bank (1970)
A company changed from tourism to pig breeding. Subsequent borrowing was ultra vires and could not be enforced by the lender.

2. The 1963 Act Changes

Section 8 of the Companies Act 1963 introduces a reform, whereby a third party must have actual knowledge of the ultra vires nature of the transaction. A legal act which is ultra vires a company is now enforceable against the company by the third party. A third party is no longer presumed to have constructive knowledge of a company's objects, but instead must be actually aware that the company lacked power before their contract will be unenforceable.

However, a person who reads a company's memorandum and misunderstands it is not protected by section 8 of the 1963 Act.

Northern Bank Finance Corporation Ltd v Quinn and Achates Investment Co (1979) Ire.

NBF lent money to Q which was guaranteed by A. NBF's solicitor had read A's memorandum before accepting them as guarantor.

Held: The bank could not rely on section 8 as they did not come within the scope of someone who was 'not . . . actually aware' of the objects of Achates Investment Co. Thus the guarantee was ultra vires and unenforceable.

Re Frederick Inns Ltd (in liquidation) (1994) Ire.

Four companies in a group of ten went into liquidation. The liquidator discovered that the holding company had paid €1.5 million to the Revenue Commissioners for the ten companies.

Held: The payment of tax for a subsidiary company was ultra vires, because there was nothing in the memorandum of association of the holding company to allow it. The Revenue Commissioners could not rely on the protection of section 8, because the payment of another company's tax liabilities could not have been 'lawfully and effectively' done pursuant to section 8, and the Revenue Commissioners had to repay the tax paid for the six other companies to the liquidator. (The money was deemed to be held on a 'constructive trust' by the Revenue Commissioners, ie not an actual trust, but one that is constructed or assumed.)

3. *EC Regulations 1973*

Article 6, EC (Companies) Regulations 1973 also applies to ultra vires contracts made by the directors. If such a contract is made in good faith it will be enforceable against a company which lacks power.

This is less frequently used than section 8, CA 1963 because it only applies to the actions of directors and can only be used in relation to limited companies. The test of 'good faith' may have resulted in a different outcome in *Northern Bank Finance*, but because Achates Investment Co had unlimited liability, article 6 could not be used by the bank.

4. *The Effects of an Ultra Vires Contract*

1. An ultra vires contract is void and unenforceable by a company.
2. A third party may enforce the contract under section 8, CA 1963 and article 6, EC Regulations 1973.

3. Directors may be restrained by an injunction from making an ultra vires contract and have to compensate the company for any such contract (see *Parke v Daily News Ltd*).

5. Ultra Vires Gifts

The rules in relation to ultra vires gifts can be stated as follows:
1. An object or power to make gifts will be valid if it is expressed in the memorandum.
2. An object or power to make gifts can be implied in the memorandum, but it must be for the benefit of the company as a whole.

Parke v Daily News Ltd (1961)
Held: A redundancy gift of €2 million to the employees did not benefit the company, ie the shareholders, as a whole, and was thus ultra vires.

Evans v Brunner Mond Ltd (1921)
Held: Gifts to universities for scientific research from a chemical company were intra vires, as there was potential benefit to the company.

Re Lee Behrens & Co (1932)
Held: A pension to the widow of a former director was ultra vires as there was no benefit to the company.

Simmonds v Heffer (1982)
Held: A donation of €63,500 by an anti-bloodsports group to the English Labour Party's election fund was ultra vires as it was not for the obvious benefit of the group. However, a gift of €38,000 to promote anti-bloodsports legislation was intra vires.

Altering the Memorandum

1. The name clause – can be altered by special resolution and with the consent of the Minister.
2. The objects clause – can be altered by special resolution. However, 15 per cent of the shareholders can object to the alteration in Court within twenty-one days, provided that they did not agree with the alteration at the initial vote.
3. The capital clause – varying rules depend on the type of alteration being made (see chapter 5).
4. The limited liability clause – a company can change from being limited to unlimited by the written consent of all the members.

Articles of Association

The articles of association are the internal rules and regulations of the company. Table A is the standard set adopted by companies. It is a schedule to the CA 1963. The articles of association must be signed by the subscribers, and are registered along with the other documentation. In a case of conflict, where the memorandum says one thing and the articles say another, the memorandum prevails as the more important document.

Some examples of what the articles contains are procedural issues like the transfer of shares (see chapter 6); power and duties of directors (see chapter 11); general meetings (see chapter 13).

Once the articles are registered, they are deemed to create a legally binding contract between the shareholders and the company under section 25, CA 1963.

The articles can be enforced as a contract:

- by the members against the company
- by the company against the members
- by the members against each other.

Alteration of the Articles

The articles of association can be altered by a special resolution of the members, subject to the provisions of the Act and the memorandum, as provided for by section 15, CA 1963.

However, there are a number of limitations on this freedom of alteration. An alteration:

- cannot overrule the Companies Acts
- cannot overrule the memorandum
- cannot overrule the general law of the State.

In addition, a company cannot bind itself not to alter its articles at a later date, although to do so may lead to a breach of contract.

Although the law allows alterations of a company's articles, it has been held that there is a strict requirement that the alteration must be bona fide (genuine) and in the best interests of the company as a whole, as in *Greenhalgh v Arderne Cinema* (1951).

The courts are particularly suspicious of an alteration which has the effect of expelling a member from the company (*Sidebotham v Kershaw, Leese & Co Ltd* (1920)).

Shuttleworth v Cox Bros (Maidenhead) Ltd (1927)
Held: The removal of a director for life was acceptable because the director had continually failed to account for money which he had received on behalf of the company.

The removal of a member may give rise to an action for oppression under section 205, CA 1963 (see chapter 14).

5

SHARE CAPITAL

The Capital and Finance of a Company

A company's capital is the money it has available to trade with, the basic funding of the company. Capital can be share capital and loan capital. ('Loan capital' which is in fact borrowing rather than capital, is considered in chapter 9.)

Share Capital

A company can raise capital by borrowing from personal investors or financial institutions, by a rights issue, gearing, or getting state aid and grants. Also, as seen in the previous chapter, a company needs an object or power to borrow, and will usually also need security.

Types of Capital

There are different types of capital:

1. Nominal or Authorised Capital

This is the total amount of shares which the company has authority to issue, either when it is formed or at a later date.

2. Issued or Allotted Capital

This is the nominal value of shares which the company has actually issued. A company need not allot all of its share capital, and very often there is a difference between the nominal/authorised share capital which a company is allowed to issue and the issued/allotted share capital which it has actually issued, eg a private company might have an authorised capital of €10,000, but an issued capital of only €1,000. The rest of the capital is called the unissued capital. (A reference to a company's capital generally means the issued share capital.)

3. Called-up or Paid-up Capital

This is the value of shares which members have paid up to date, where shares are being paid for in instalments. The remaining money per share which each shareholder owes the company is known as the 'uncalled capital'. (In practice, most shares are fully paid for on purchase, so there is rarely any uncalled capital.)

4. Reserve Capital

This is uncalled capital which is reserved for a special purpose. Under section 67, CA 1963, a company may pass a special resolution stating that some or all of the uncalled capital may only be called up when the company is being wound up. (This puts the company in a position similar to that of a company limited by guarantee, in relation to the reserve capital.)

Alteration of the Capital Clause

According to section 68, CA 1963, a limited company, if authorised by its articles, may in a general meeting make the following alterations to its capital clause:

1. Increase its share capital, eg a company might increase its capital from €1,000 shares to €2,000, by creating 1,000 new €1 shares.
2. Consolidate existing shares into shares of larger nominal value, eg two 50c shares might be consolidated into one €1 share.
3. Divide existing shares into shares of smaller nominal value, eg one €5 share might be divided into five €1 shares.
4. Cancel unissued shares and reduce the authorised share capital, eg a company might have an authorised share capital of €10,000 in €1 shares, of which €7,000 is issued. The company could then cancel up to €3,000 in unissued shares and reduce its authorised share capital to €7,000. (Note that if a company wishes to reduce its issued/allotted share capital, it must go through the reduction of capital procedure explained in chapter 7.)
5. Convert paid-up shares into stock and reconvert that stock into paid-up shares of any denomination.

Table A Article 44 provides that a company may make these alterations by way of an ordinary resolution. Section 69, CA 1963 requires that a company must inform the registrar of companies within one month of altering its share capital.

Raising Share Capital

A public company can issue shares in the following ways:

-   An offer for sale to the public – this is where new shares are sold through an issuing house, which then sells them to the public. The issuing house underwrites the issue, ie they buy all the shares even though they may not sell them all. (This is to avoid the risk of failing to reach the required minimum subscription.)
-   A placing – this is where the new shares are placed with or allotted to an issuing house, which then places (or sells) the shares to private investors.
-   A rights issue – this is where new shares are offered to existing shareholders on a pre-emption basis, ie in proportion to their existing shareholding
-   An open offer – this is where new shares are offered to existing shareholders who may buy as many or as a few as they like.

(Remember that a private company cannot invite the public to buy its shares under section 21, C(A)A 1983.)

Allotment of Shares

The original allotment occurs when a company is formed and the subscribers agree in the memorandum to take shares. Subsequently, when a company decides to allot shares, it is creating and selling new shares for the first time. The allotment of shares is an increase in the company's capital.

The allotment of shares is a binding contract between the company and the new subscriber. Once the new subscriber is entered onto the register of members, he or she will be legally a member of the company. The issue of shares is when the subscriber receives their share certificate, ie the issuing of shares follows naturally from the allotment. Shares may be allotted at a premium, but not at a discount.

Issuing Shares at a Premium

All shares have a nominal or par value which is usually expressed in small denominations, eg €1. Shares may be allotted at a premium, ie above their par value. The excess must be paid into the share premium account, eg a successful company may allot new €1 shares for €1.30 – the 30c is the share premium. This premium is not part of trading profits of the company and according to section 62, CA 1963, can only be used for:

- paying up unissued shares for use in a bonus issue (a gift of shares to existing shareholders which converts the premium into share capital)
- writing off preliminary expenses of the company
- paying any premium due on redemption of redeemable preference shares (see chapter 6).

Issuing Shares at a Discount

Shares may not be allotted at a discount. This is to protect the capital for creditors. Thus, a €1 share may not be allotted for 70c.

Ooregum Gold Mining v Roper (1892)

€1.27 shares were allotted for 32c.
Held: The company could not validly issue shares at a discount, and the person who got the discount must repay it to the company plus 5 per cent interest.

Section 27, C(A)A 1983 provides that 'shares of a company shall not be allotted at a discount'. However, there are also exceptions in section 27:

1. A private company allotting shares for a non-cash consideration may 'honestly and reasonably' overvalue the asset which is consideration, eg if Z Ltd issues €5,000 of shares in return for a second-hand van, it does not matter if the van is only worth €4,000 if the inaccurate evaluation was honest and reasonable.
2. Payment of commission. If shares are issued through a broker, the broker may take up to 10 per cent commission, provided there is authority to do so in the articles and the commission is disclosed in the prospectus.

The procedure on the allotment of shares is that the new shareholder's name must be entered onto the register of members, and he or she is issued with a share certificate.

Restrictions on Allotment

The Companies (Amendment) Act 1983 introduced a number of restrictions on when a company may allot new shares.

(a) Directors Must Have Permission to Allot

Section 20, C(A)A 1983 states that directors must have authority to allot, given by:

– the company in general meeting, or
– the articles of the company.

Section 20 also provides that the authority must state:

– the maximum amount of shares which may be allotted, and
– the term of the allotment, which must not exceed five years.

There are exceptions in the section, for:

– shares taken by original subscribers and
– shares taken under employee share schemes.

If directors allot shares without authority, the allotment is valid but the directors can be fined €25,000 for knowingly breaching the regulations.

(b) Pre-emption Under Section 23, C(A)A 1983

A company which is allotting ordinary shares ('equity securities') must first offer them to existing shareholders in the same proportion as their existing holding. This allows shareholders to keep their level of shareholding constant. Pre-emption is also known as a rights issue.

The right of pre-emption may be removed by the company. A private company can permanently exclude pre-emption in either their memorandum or articles, or pass a special resolution. A public company can only remove the right by special resolution.

(c) Allotment of Shares for Non-cash Consideration in PLCs

The Companies (Amendment) Act 1983 introduced strict rules on when shares in a public company could be purchased for a non-cash purchase price:

– Under section 26, C(A)A 1983 if the consideration for the shares is work or services, the work or services must be performed before the allotment (in case it might not be forthcoming after the shares have been allotted). However, goodwill and expertise are both acceptable as consideration.
– Under section 29, C(A)A 1983 if the consideration is an undertaking or promise to perform an act, that undertaking must be performed within five years.
– Under section 30, C(A)A 1983 if the consideration is a non cash asset, the asset must be valued by an independent valuer, within six

months prior to the allotment. The valuation must be done by someone who is a qualified auditor.

If any of these sections are breached, the allottee may be personally liable to the company and an officer of the company who is in default of the above provisions shall be guilty of an offence. If a company contravenes section 26 or section 29, the allottee must pay the company the nominal value of the shares plus any premium.

Allotment of Shares by a Public Company

A public company must have a minimum paid-up share capital of €38,100, with at least 25 per cent paid up, according to section 28, C(A)A 1983. In addition to this, there are three major limitations on the power of a public company to allot shares:

(a) Minimum Subscription

Under section 53, CA 1963 there must be a minimum response to the public invitation to subscribe for shares. The directors must state the minimum amount which must be raised by the public subscription to ensure that the company has satisfied the public that it has sufficient investment before proceeding with the public flotation. If the minimum subscription is not raised within forty days of the issue of the prospectus, any money received for shares must be repaid. PLCs use underwriters to avoid the risk of failing to reach the minimum subscription.

Section 22, C(A)A 1983 further provides that a plc may not allot shares unless

– the capital is subscribed in full, or
– the offer states that if it is not subscribed in full the amount of the capital subscribed may be allotted in any event or in the event of specified conditions being satisfied.

If an allotment is made contrary to either section, the directors may be made personally liable to repay any money received plus 5 per cent interest.

(b) No allotment Until a Specified Period After Issue of Prospectus

Section 56, CA 1963 provides that no allotment can be made until the fourth day (or longer) after the issue of the prospectus. This is to allow potential investors time to consider investing.

(c) Permission from the Stock Exchange

Under section 57, CA 1963 if a company states that permission has or will be sought to deal shares on the Stock Exchange, then permission must be sought within three days of the issue of the prospectus, or any allotment of shares will be void. Equally any allotment will be void if permission has not been granted within six months of the closing of the subscription lists.

6

SHARES

Nature of Shares

Shares were defined in *Borland's Trustee v Steel Bros & Co Ltd* (1901) as 'the interest of a shareholder in a company measured by a sum of money, for the purposes of liability in the first place, and of interest in the second'. This means that shares determine the amount of money still owed to a company in the case of partly paid shares, and the amount of dividends payable. Shares are also a contract between a company and its shareholders, consisting of a series of rights and obligations.

Types of Shares

A company's memorandum may create different classes of shares:

Preference Shares

A preference share usually gives the shareholder one or both of two main rights:

1. a prior right to receive a fixed dividend, for example at 10 per cent, and
2. the right to a return of capital in the winding-up of a company in priority to other shareholders.

Preference shareholders usually cannot vote at general meetings.

Ordinary Shares

All other shares are ordinary shares, by far the most common in Irish companies. These shareholders generally have the right to vote and receive a fluctuating dividend.

Redeemable Shares

Redeemable shares are a type of share which the company issues with the intention of redeeming them (or buying them back) at a later date. As such, redeemable shares constitute an exception to the rule that a company may not purchase its own shares.

Under section 207, CA 1990, the rules on redeemable shares are as follows:

1. At least one tenth of the company's issued share capital is non-redeemable.
2. Redeemable shares may only be redeemed when they are fully paid.
3. Redeemable shares may only be redeemed out of profits which are available for distribution (so that when the share capital is reduced on cancellation of the shares, the corresponding assets are still intact).
4. If a company intends to cancel shares on redemption, they may redeem the shares out of a fresh issue of shares. (This has the effect that the share capital remains the same.)
5. If a company pays a shareholder a premium on redemption of redeemable preference shares, the premium must be paid out of profits available for distribution. The one exception to this is if the shares were originally issued at a premium, and are to be redeemed out of proceeds of a fresh issue of shares, then the premium is to be paid out of the share premium account.
6. If shares are cancelled on redemption, the company's issued share capital can be reduced by the nominal value of the redeemed shares, but an equivalent amount must be transferred to the 'Capital Redemption Reserve Fund', which is treated as capital (and subject to same rules on reduction).

If shares are not cancelled they must be retained as 'Treasury Shares'. These shares keep the capital the same, but are effectively frozen as shareholders have no rights to vote or dividends. These shares can later be reissued. Only 10 per cent of shares may be treasury.

Shareholders' Rights

The rights of shareholders depend on the class or type of share they hold. Class rights are those attaching to a particular class. Class rights may be varied as set out in section 38, C(A)A 1983. The variation depends on whether the right is stated in the memorandum or articles, and whether there is a procedure provided.

Section 38, C(A)A 1983 provides:

1. Rights and procedures in memorandum or articles: where the right is in the company's memorandum or articles and a variation procedure is stated, and the variation concerns

– the directors' authority to allot shares under section 20, CA 1963
– a reduction of capital under section 72, CA 1963

the agreement of 75 per cent of the shareholders is required.

The holders of 10 per cent of the shares may challenge the variation in court within twenty-eight days, provided they did not previously vote for the variation.

2. Right in memorandum and no procedures: if the right is in the memorandum and no procedure is stated, the agreement of all members of the company is needed.
3. Right in articles and no procedures: if the right is in the articles and no procedure is stated, the agreement of 75 per cent of the shareholders is needed (subject to the right of 10 per cent to challenge the variation in court within twenty-one days).

In all cases agreement can be by consent in writing or by special resolution.

Transmission and Transfer of Shares

Where shares are passed from one holder to another, proper procedures must be followed. Transmission is an involuntary process, ie it involves the registration in the names of a personal representative after the death of a shareholder, or a shareholder's assignees in the case of bankruptcy. This person may then become a member if the shares are registered in his/her name under section 81, CA 1963, or he/she may see that the shares are transferred to another person.

The transfer of shares is a voluntary process where a shareholder decides to sell, or make a gift of, all or part of their shares, to another person. In order to legally transfer shares, a proper instrument of transfer must be used and stamp duty must be paid.

A transfer can be by one of two methods:

1. A simple transfer is where the owner is transferring all his shares together.
2. A certified transfer is where the owner transfers part of his shareholding.

Director's Discretion to Refuse Transfers

In a private company the directors will usually have the discretion to refuse to register a transfer, or specify when the directors may refuse a transfer. The power to refuse a transfer is a fiduciary power of the directors, which must be exercised in good faith in the best interests of the company as a whole.

Re Hackney Pavillion Ltd (1924)
Two directors disagreed on a transfer. No decision was made and the secretary informed the deceased's executors that the transfer had been refused.
Held: This was untrue, as an actual act of refusal is necessary. The court ordered rectification of the register of members by registering the transfer.

Re Smith & Fawcett Ltd (1942)
The directors refused a transfer to a deceased shareholder's son, exercising their 'absolute and uncontrolled discretion', but offered to transfer a lesser amount to the son.
Held: This was in the best interests of the company on the facts.

Re Hafner Olhausen v Powderly (1943) Ire.
The plaintiff's transfer was refused by the directors exercising their 'absolute and uncontrolled discretion without assigning reasons'. The Court said that while the company was entitled to refuse without reasons, the Court could draw conclusions from failure to give reasons.
Held: The discretion to refuse the transfer was not exercised in good faith for the benefit of the company as a whole.

Incorrect and Forged Transfers

The buyer becomes the legal owner of the shares when his/her name is entered onto the register of members. A share certificate is prima facie evidence of membership, and a company may be estopped from denying that the information on the share certificate is incorrect.

Bloomenthal v Ford (1897)
A company issued a share certificate which incorrectly stated that a person's shares were fully paid up.
Held: The company was estopped from denying that this statement was untrue and calling for the unpaid amounts.

The issue of forged share transfers is more complicated because a forgery is a nullity in law, and a person who relies on a forgery may be held to be personally liable on it, even though he/she is completely innocent of the forgery. If a person suffers as a result of an incorrect share certificate, the company will be liable in damages, as they are estopped from denying that the share cert is correct.

If a forged transfer is used, the company will be liable to the person who purchases the shares on the faith of the transfer.

Re Bahia (1866)
A shareholder's signature was forged on a transfer and her shares sold to a new owner.
Held: The shares were returned to the original owner, but the buyer had to be compensated as the company were estopped from denying that the transfer was correct.

A company will not be liable if the share certificate itself is a forgery, issued by a person who had no authority to do so (*Rubin v Great Fingall Consolidated Co* (1906)).

If the transferee is aware that the share certificate is incorrect, the company will not be liable.

Raising Finance on Shares

Shares are often used as security for borrowing, and commonly shares will be mortgaged as a way of raising finance. Shares may be the subject of a legal mortgage where the mortgagee or lender becomes the registered holder of the shares, with a separate agreement to re-transfer ownership on repayment of the loan. Due to the complications involved in this, such as the payment of dividends, it is rarely done in practice.

An equitable mortgage involves the deposit of the share certificate with the lender, but ownership remains with the borrower. A signed instrument of transfer is usually deposited with the share certificate, and if the borrower defaults, the lender simply fills in the transfer and sells the shares. Due to its simplicity, the equitable mortgage is much more common in practice.

Share Warrants

A share warrant is a document which states that the bearer is the owner of the shares. By section 88, CA 1963 a company limited by shares with authority in its articles may issue warrants for fully paid-up shares. Once a share warrant is delivered to another person, that other person becomes the legal owner of the shares.

Lien, Surrender and Forfeiture

The company can also exercise a lien over its members' shares for money owed to the company, if the articles allow it. This is simply a provision that gives the company first claim on the shares if the shareholder is in debt to the company.

A shareholder who has unpaid amounts on his or her shares may decide to surrender them to the company, rather than pay the outstanding amounts. Similarly, a company's articles may provide for forfeiture of shares to the company if the shareholder cannot pay the outstanding amounts on his shares.

7

CAPITAL MAINTENANCE

Principle of Capital Maintenance

The capital which the company gets from shareholders must be maintained in order to provide a 'creditor's buffer', ie a fund to which creditors can look if the company is unable to pay debts. However, in practice the invested capital may have been diminished by trading losses, or the invested capital may only be a small amount, and thus the detailed rules of maintenance are largely irrelevant.

The issues involved in capital maintenance are:

Increase of Capital

A company increases its capital where it allots new shares. This can be done by an ordinary resolution, as explained in chapter 6.

Reduction of Capital

A company may cancel its unissued shares, which reduces the authorised share capital, but this does not alter the company's overall financial position. Under section 72, CA 1963, if a company wishes to reduce its issued share capital, it may do so provided:

1. it has authority to do so in its articles of association, and
2. it passes a special resolution, and
3. it obtains Court approval for the reduction. The court's role in the reduction is to ensure creditors are not prejudiced.

The acceptable types of reductions are explained in section 72, CA 1963. These are:

- a reduction of liability on unpaid shares
- a reduction of paid-up shares which are lost or unrepresented by available assets
- repayment of paid-up share capital in excess of company wants.

Purchase by a Company of its Own Shares

The rule that a company should not purchase its own shares originated in *Trevor v Whitworth* (1887), and was prohibited in section 41, C(A)A 1983.

Section 41 as amended by section 232, CA 1990 also introduced the following exceptions where a company *may* purchase its own shares:

1. 'other than for a valuable consideration', ie as a gift
2. redemption of redeemable preference shares
3. acquisition of shares in a reduction of capital
4. under a court order, eg under section 205, CA 1963, see *Irish Press plc v Ingersoll Irish Publications Ltd* (1994) Ire. (see chapter 14)
5. forfeiture or surrender of shares.

Further exceptions were introduced by section 212, CA 1990:

6. A 'market purchase' where shares are purchased on a recognised stock exchange, subject to a marketing arrangement. This must be authorised by an ordinary resolution. A general authorisation to purchase may be given to a company if it specifies the maximum amount of shares which may be purchased, the price range and the latest date of purchase which must be within eighteen months of the general meeting.
7. An 'off market purchase' where shares are purchased other then on a recognised stock exchange, ie a purchase by a private company or an unlisted public company. This must be authorised by a special resolution in which the seller does not vote.

Assistance by a Company in the Purchase of its Own Shares

Section 60, CA 1963 prohibits a company from giving financial assistance to a person to purchase its shares 'whether directly or indirectly, and whether by means of a loan, guarantee, provision of security or otherwise'. In other words, Company Z cannot lend or give money to A to buy its shares, nor may it guarantee a bank loan to A for this purpose. The aim of this section was to prevent people from taking over companies by using the companies' own resources. But section 60 catches much more than that.

There is no requirement as to the form a loan may take – assistance may be direct or indirect.

Charterhouse Investment Trust Ltd v Tempest Diesels Ltd (1987)
Held: One must look at the commercial realities of a transaction to
decide if a company has given financial assistance.

This test was applied in Ireland in:

Re CH (Ireland) Inc (1997) Ire.
A complex circle of transactions involving two companies and their
subsidiaries began with CHI depositing €22,800,000 in a Swiss bank
account and ended with a subsidiary buying €22,800,000 worth of
shares in CHI.
Held: This was giving assistance within section 60, as the main
purpose of making the deposit was to assist in acquiring shares.

The exceptions under section 60, CA 1963 are:

1. All companies can:

    – lend money in connection with employee share schemes
    – lend money in the ordinary course of business
    – lend money to bona fide non-director employees.

2. A private company may lend money to a prospective shareholder
    if they pass a special resolution and make a statutory declaration.
    This statutory declaration, made by two directors, must state:

    – the form of such assistance
    – the name of the person given assistance
    – the intended purpose of the assistance, and
    – the fact that the company is solvent.

A dissenting ten per cent of shareholders may petition the High Court
for cancellation of the assistance within twenty-eight days.
    The court requires strict compliance with section 60 procedures:

Re Northside Motor Co Ltd (1985) Ire.
A company guaranteed a loan for the purpose of allowing a 50 per
cent shareholder to acquire more shares with the full knowledge of its
bank. The bank then realised that section 60 procedures had not been
followed and the company belatedly passed a statutory declaration
and special resolution. Later a liquidator sought to recover money
paid under the guarantee.
Held: These steps should be done prior to assistance, not after. Thus
there was a breach of section 60.

Lombard & Ulster Banking Ltd v Bank of Ireland (1987) Ire.
Prospective purchasers of the majority of company X borrowed money from L&U. Company X guaranteed the loan and gave company property as security. There was no statutory declaration or special resolution, only an informal agreement of all shareholders to permit the transaction.
Held: Not sufficient under section 60.

Transactions in breach of section 60 are voidable by a company against a person who had notice of the facts.
  In all companies, private or public, section 60, CA 1963 does not prohibit assistance which takes the form of:

- payment of a properly declared dividend
- discharge of a lawfully incurred liability
- lending money in ordinary course of business
- loans to bona fide non-director employees
- loans in connection with employee share schemes.

Effect of Breach

Section 60 states that any transaction in breach is voidable at the instance of the company against any person who had notice of the facts constituting a breach.

Bank of Ireland Ltd v Rockfield Ltd (1979) Ire.
Held: 'Notice' in section 60 means actual notice, not constructive notice.

In *Re Northside Motor Co Ltd* (1985) Ire., the guarantee under section 60 was ineffective because the bank had notice of all the circumstances.

Also, if a company gives assistance by way of an unlawful loan, the contract is illegal and the money lent cannot be recovered. If a company suffers loss as a result, the directors can be sued as constructive trustees of the money.
  There is also a criminal sanction for officers who breach section 60.

Meeting re Serious Loss of Capital

Under section 40, C(A)A 1983, if the net assets of a company are half or less of the company's called-up share capital, the directors must convene a meeting of the company to discuss this serious loss of capital. This will be discussed in chapter 16 on meetings.

8

SHARE RELATED ISSUES – DIVIDENDS AND INSIDER DEALING

Distribution Of Profits

A shareholder normally invests in a company in the hope of making a profit at a later date. There are two main ways of making such a profit – selling the shares at a profit, or earning dividends on the shares.

A shareholder generally has the right to earn dividends, ie periodic payments of money which represent the company's profits. The payment of dividends are regulated by the company's memorandum and articles, and by legal rules.

Declaration of Dividend

A company has an implied right to declare a dividend, but it is usually dealt with in the articles of association. Under Table A:

1. A dividend must be declared by the company in general meeting. This declaration cannot exceed the amount recommended by the directors.
2. The directors may also declare an interim dividend as they see fit.
3. A shareholder is not entitled to a dividend unless it has been declared according to the articles and the date for payment has arrived. Thus preference shareholders are only entitled to their dividend when their specified date of payment arrives.
4. The directors may, before paying dividends, set aside profits to be used for other purposes. This is a management decision, ie a company does not have to pay a dividend and cannot be compelled to do so according to *Bond v Barrow Hematite Steel Co* (1902).
5. Dividends are declared as payable on paid up amounts of shares only, ie if shares are only 50 per cent partly paid, then 50 per cent of the full dividend will be paid.

6. Dividends are paid in cash only, unless the company provides otherwise. Dividends paid other than in cash are known as paid *in specie*.
7. Dividends shall only be paid in accordance with Part IV of the Companies (Amendment) Act 1983.

Part IV of the Companies (Amendment) Act 1983

The key provisions of C(A)A 1983 are sections 45 and 46.

Under section 45:
1. Dividends must be paid out of the profits available for the distribution. In other words, dividends cannot be paid out of a company's capital, as this would be an unauthorised reduction of capital.

   According to section 45, the profits available for distribution are 'a company's accumulated realised profits, so far as not previously utilised by distribution or capitalisation, less its accumulated realised losses, so far as not previously written off in a reduction or reorganisation of capital duly made'.

2. A company must be solvent, that is in a position to pay its debts as they fall due, before a dividend can be paid.

Section 46, C(A)A 1983 provides that, in relation to a public limited company, a dividend can only be paid if its net assets are not less than the aggregate of the called-up share capital and undistributable reserves, and the distribution does not reduce the amount of those assets to less than the aggregate amount.

'Undistributable reserves' are:

- the share premium account
- the capital redemption reserve fund
- any surplus of accumulated unrealised profits over accumulated unrealised losses
- any reserve which the company's memorandum or articles prohibit it from distributing.

Companies which have suffered a significant loss of capital, but are trading profitably on what remains, can use section 72, CA 1963 to reduce their capital in order to be in a position to pay a dividend, as explained in chapter 7.

Additional Points

Special rules apply to investment companies under section 47, C(A)A 1983, and to assurance companies under section 48, C(A)A 1983.

The onus is on a company's accountant to determine whether a dividend should be paid, by consulting properly prepared relevant accounts. Failure to do so may give rise to liability in negligence.

If an unlawful distribution is made by a company to a member who has reasonable grounds to believe it was unlawful, the company may recover the money.

If a company with an unpaid cumulative dividend goes into liquidation, the preference shareholders are not entitled to a dividend, unless this is provided for in the articles of association, or the dividend has been declared but not paid when the company goes into liquidation.

Insider Dealing

Insider dealing (or insider trading) is where people with confidential price-sensitive information, acquired by an inside connection to a company, use that information to make profits for themselves or others, by dealing in securities with people not privy to the information.

Before 1990 it was only unethical, but it has been prohibited in Ireland since the Companies Act 1990, which was inspired by an EU Commission directive prohibiting categories of insider dealing.

Unlawful Dealings by Insiders

An 'insider' is a person who is or was connected with the company within the previous six months, in possession of 'relevant information'. A 'person connected with the company' has been widely defined and includes officers, shareholders and people in business relations with a company such as solicitors or auditors. A 'primary insider' is the person connected to the company, and a 'secondary insider' is someone who receives information from a primary insider.

'Dealing' covers acquiring, disposing, underwriting, offering, making agreements in relation to shares, and attempting or inducing another to do so.

'Securities' covers shares and debentures, which are proposed or issued in Ireland or elsewhere, and quoted on a recognised stock exchange.

Section 108, CA 1990

Section 108(1), 1990 states that it is unlawful for a person to deal with company securities, if he or she was connected with the company within the past six months and is in possession of information likely to affect the share price if it was generally available.

Section 108(2) states that it is unlawful for a person to deal with company securities if he or she is connected to another company and is in possession of confidential price-sensitive information about an actual/contemplated/cancelled transaction of one or both companies.

Section 108(3) states that it is unlawful for a person to deal with company securities based on information from an 'insider' prohibited under (1) or (2).

Sections 108(4) and (5) state that it is unlawful for an insider prohibited under (1) or (2) to cause another to deal in securities.

Civil Sanction

Section 109, CA 1990 states that a person found to be dealing as an insider must compensate any other party to the transaction who was not in possession of relevant information for any loss, ie difference in price between what securities dealt at and what they would have been if the other party had had the information. Also, the dealer must account to the company for any profit accruing from dealing in securities.

The amount of compensation is the actual profit or loss minus any amount already paid by the 'insider' to the other as a result of the same transaction. An action under section 109 must be brought within two years of completion of the transaction.

Criminal Sanction

Section 111, CA 1990 provides the following sanctions:

- on summary conviction – 12 months imprisonment and/or €1,270 fine
- on indictment – 10 years imprisonment and/or €254,000 fine
- plus a 12-month ban on dealing.

Supervising the Act

Under section 115, CA 1990 the Stock Exchange has a duty to report suspected or actual insider dealing to the Director of Corporate Enforcement. The directors, other management and members of the Stock Exchange must report their knowledge or suspicions to the Exchange. Alternatively, a person interested in the proceeding may apply to the court to direct the relevant authority to make a report.

To enable it to report to the Director of Corporate Enforcement, the manager of the Exchange may investigate suspected insider dealing by requiring a person to give information about securities, dealings, the issuing company or any other information. Either side can apply to court for a declaration that the common good justifies or does not justify the use of this power. Failure to comply with a court order is contempt.

The Stock Exchange must also present an annual report to the Minister for Enterprise, Trade and Employment, giving details of complaints and reports and investigations which did not lead to reports. This report is also laid before the Oireachtas.

As a result of the EU origins of this part of the 1990 Act, section 116 imposes a duty of co-operation on stock exchanges within the member states. Before answering such a request, the stock exchange must advise the Minister, who may disallow a reply if:

(a) criminal or civil proceedings have commenced in Ireland
(b) a person has been convicted in Ireland in relation to this case
(c) the case would adversely affect security, sovereignty or public policy of the state.

Exempt Transactions

Under section 110, CA 1990, the following transactions are exempt:

– inherited securities
– employee profit-sharing schemes
– bona fide transactions by personal representatives of parties
– bona fide transactions from mortgages/charges on shares
– bona fide acquisitions of shares by a director.

Caselaw

Of the handful of insider-dealing cases, both criminal and civil, to have come before the High Court, none have been successful.

DPP v Byrne (2002) Ire.
Held: Criminal intent must be proven in a prosecution for insider dealing. The accused must have had price-sensitive information and the intention to profit from using that information.

Fyffes plc v Flavin (2005) Ire.
In this long-running civil case on insider dealing, the plaintiff plc failed to prove insider dealing by their former director.
Held: The defendant was not in possession of price-sensitive information.

Private Companies

The 1990 Act applies only to public companies listed on the Stock Exchange.

Private companies are regulated by directors' fiduciary duties, and also legislative provisions, ie section 30, CA 1990 prohibits directors from dealing in the company's shares and debentures; section 59, CA 1990 requires a company to keep a register of directors' and secretaries' shares and interests.

9

COMPANY BORROWING

Companies have an implied power to borrow and usually an express power to borrow too.

A company will also have the power to give security for borrowing, either express or implied, by way of a legal or equitable mortgage. Companies may borrow from various sources, e.g. personal investors and financial institutions. (For ultra vires borrowing, see chapter 4; for director's authority to borrow, see chapter 11.)

Shares versus Debentures

A number of essential legal differences are involved in the company's decision as to which form of security to issue:

1. A shareholder is an *owner* of the company, whereas a debenture holder is a *creditor*.
2. On liquidation, debts to debenture holders are repaid in advance of repayments to shareholders.
3. The interest that a company pays on a debenture is tax deductable, which makes it attractive to a company.
4. A company may purchase its own debentures (unless the debenture provides otherwise). Redeemed debentures may be reissued.
5. A company may only pay dividends to shareholders out of profits; interest is due on debentures whether or not there is any profit.

Debentures

Most loans are by way of debentures. A debenture is a document acknowledging a debt by a company. A debenture usually provides security, or a charge, which the lender can enforce by way of receivership if the debts fall into arrears.

Types of debentures

(a) A Single Debenture
A single debenture is the most common type in Ireland. It is an individual loan made to a company.

(b) A Series of Debentures

A series of debentures is a group of separate loans issued on standard conditions, done to raise a total amount. The key condition is that all the debentures rank equally (or *pari passu*), although the loans may be created on different dates.

(c) Debenture Stock

Debenture stock is where a large group of lenders subscribe for debentures and the loan is treated as part of an overall stock figure. It is used by public companies to raise finance from the public at large, and for convenience all the loans are treated as part of a fictional overall figure. Each loan may be split into amounts, eg €10, and is transferable.

Debenture Trust Deed

A debenture trust deed may be used with a series of debentures and debenture stock.

It is a legal document which appoints a trustee to act on behalf of all the debenture holders, to enforce the security and appoint the receiver. A debenture trust deed usually contains:

1. the name and address of the trustee
2. provision for the payment of the trustee
3. a statement that the trustee represents the interests of the debenture holder
4. an undertaking by the company to repay the loan and interest at specified times
5. the creation of a legal mortgage on the company's assets which form the security
6. a statement of when these securities may be enforced
7. the authorisation of the trustee to enforce the security and appoint a receiver in case of default
8. an undertaking by the company to maintain and insure the charged property
9. detailed provisions dealing with a register of debenture stock-holders, meeting of debenture holders, issue of certificates, transfer of stock etc.

Advantages of Debenture Trust Deed

The advantages of a debenture trust deed are:

1. If a fixed charge is created, no later lender can obtain prior right to repayment.

2. Speed – the trustee can act quicker than a group of individual debenture holders.
3. Convenience – individual debenture holders do not have to liase with each other or supervise their investment.

However, the debenture trust deed is an additional cost to the debenture holder.

Transferability of Debentures

A debenture is transferable according to the terms of the debenture itself. There are also bearer debentures which are payable to the bearer. These are transferred by delivery, in the same way as share warrants.

There are also convertible debentures which may be converted into shares in the company at a specified rate of exchange. These are used where investors would be slow to buy shares in a company which may not make profits for some time to come. (There is no ban on a company issuing debentures at a discount.)

Register of Debenture Holders

The company must keep a register of debenture holders, under section 91, CA 1963. The register must contain the names and addresses of the debenture holders and the amount of debentures held by each. The register must be kept at the company's registered office, or at another place notified to the Registrar of Companies.

Company Charges

Debentures may be unsecured, but are usually secured by charges. The secured creditor has a charge over the company's assets and can enforce prior payment of his or her debts by appointing a receiver over those assets. Charges may be fixed or floating. There is also a hybrid clause, a fixed charge over book debts.

A Fixed Charge

This charge attaches to a specific asset like property, and the borrowing company cannot deal with the charged assets without the consent of the chargeholder. A fixed charge can be by way of legal or equitable mortgage over the asset. The big advantage of the fixed charge is that it ranks in priority over a floating charge when it comes to repayment.

Advantages of Fixed Charges

1. Fixed charges are the first charge to be repaid.
2. Charged assets are easily identifiable.

Disadvantages of Fixed Charges

It may be difficult for a receiver to dispose of assets at their book price because of devaluation and poor market conditions.

A Floating Charge

This is a charge which does not attach to specific assets until crystallisation. It is an equitable charge. Floating charges were defined in *Re Yorkshire Woolcombers Association Ltd* (1903) as having three features:

– a charge on a class of assets of a company present and future
– which class is, in the ordinary course of the company business, changing from time to time
– until the holder enforces the charge, the company may carry on business and deal with the charged assets.

However, a charge can still be a floating charge if it does not have all three characteristics.

Welch v Bowmaker (Ireland) and Bank of Ireland (1980) Ire.
A floating charge was created over land, which is not an asset that changes from time to time.
Held: This could still be a valid floating charge.

A floating charge is typically created over stock or book debts, which are changing assets with which the company carries on business. Floating charges are usually created by companies who have already created fixed charges on all suitable assets, or where the company does not have any asset suitable for the creation of fixed charges.

A floating charge 'floats' over the class of assets, such as stock, without affixing to any specific part of the asset. If the debt which a floating charge secures is paid, the charge simply ceases to exist. However, if the security has to be enforced, the floating charge is said to 'crystallise', at which point it affixes to whatever part of the asset is available at that time.

A floating charge crystallises:

- on the liquidation of a company
- on the appointment of a receiver to the company
- when the parties stipulate (although some academic debate surrounds this point)
- on the cessation of the company's business. This includes the sale of a company's business.

Re The Real Meat Co Ltd (1995) Ire.
Held: The sale of the business was a cessation of business which caused the floating charge to crystallise automatically.

A floating charge which crystallises on the appointment of a receiver becomes a floating charge again on the appointment of an examiner (*Re Holidair Ltd* (1994) Ire.).

Advantages of Floating Charge

1. Assets subject to a floating charge may be easier to dispose of than assets subject to a fixed charge, eg disposability of stock versus buildings.
2. It may be the only option open to a company which has no fixed assets, or fixed assets which are already subject to charges.

Disadvantages of a Floating Charge

1. Assets subject to a floating charge rank third in priority for payment, after fixed charges and preferential debts.
2. The precise value of the security is uncertain until crystallisation occurs.
3. They cannot take effect over goods which the company does not yet own, such as goods under a retention of title clause, or goods held under a hire purchase agreement.
4. A receiver can invalidate a floating charge in a number of ways:

    – if a charge is not registered under section 99, CA 1963
    – if a charge is a fraudulent preference under section 286, CA 1963
    – if a charge is created within one year of a company going into insolvent liquidation under section 288, CA 1963.

Fixed Charge over Book Debts

A fixed charge over book debts is a hybrid charge. It is quite permissible to create a floating charge over book debts, but such a charge still ranks third after fixed charges and preferential debts. In the 1980s, banks preferred to create such charges as fixed charges to take priority over preferential debts. However, the Revenue Commissioners objected to such charges because they took priority over debts to the Revenue Commissioners. Such schemes usually provided that the borrower was to collect the debts and keep them in a special bank account which would be frozen at a particular level. These are sometimes know as *Siebe Gorman* clauses, after *Siebe Gorman v Barclay's Bank Ltd* (1977). They were accepted in Ireland by the Supreme Court in *Re Keenan Brothers* (1985) Ire. However, the Court ruled that the charge could only attach to uncollected debts, as collected debts would cease to exist.

Since section 115, Finance Act 1986, the holder of a fixed charge over book debts is liable to pay the borrower's debts to the Revenue Commissioners, if the company fails to pay. Thus, the Revenue Commissioners have priority over fixed charges over book debts, so they are rarely created anymore. However, this provision led to difficulties for small companies seeking to borrow from banks. As a result, section 174, Finance Act 1995 provides that section 115 does not apply where 'within twenty-one days of the creation of the fixed charge, the holder of the charge furnishes the Revenue Commissioners with a copy of the charge to be registered under section 99, CA 1963'.

Re Holidair Ltd (1994) Ire.
Holidair Ltd sought the protection of the appointment of an examiner for itself and eighteen related companies, known as the Kentz Group. A bank claimed that Holidair Ltd had created a fixed charge over book debts in its favour in 1984, and thus the examiner could not borrow without their consent.
Supreme Court Held: The 1984 charge over book debts was a floating charge, as it was a class of assets which changed from time to time and the companies were free to draw monies from these bank accounts. Also Held: A floating charge which had crystallised on the appointment of a receiver would begin to float again on the appointment of an examiner.

Registration of Charges

Section 99, CA 1963 provides that a company must register charges with the Registrar of Companies within twenty-one days of the creation of the charge. Nine types of charges must be registered, which cover almost every type of asset.

If a charge is not registered, the charge is void and the debt it secures is repayable immediately. Thus, although the primary obligation to register is on the borrowing company, the lender should in practice ensure that the charge is registered as required, although the lender is not obliged to do so.

The company is not required to keep a register of charges, but must keep copies of every instrument of charge which requires registration at its offices. There is an important difference here, because the list of charges to be registered under section 99 is not exhaustive, so it is possible that a charge which defeats a later lender need not be registered or recorded, and the later lender is thus unaware of it.

When the Registrar issues a certificate of registration, that is conclusive evidence of compliance with the requirements of company law.

Late Registration

Charges must be registered within twenty-one days, but an extension of time may be given by the court under section 106, CA 1963 if the delay was 'accidental or due to inadvertence' and the extension is not prejudicial to any party, such as the creditors, shareholders or company. If an extension of time is granted, it is usually subject to a proviso that registration is not to effect the rights of parties who acquired rights before the actual time of registration.

Re Telford Motors Ltd (1978) Ire.
Held: The court set aside later registration of a charge because unsecured creditors had acquired rights prior to the registration and were entitled to protection.

Priority of Charges

The basic order of priority for the payment of debts is:

1. Fixed charges – rank in order of creation, ie oldest charges first.
2. Preferential debts – all rank equally (or *pari passu*).
3. Floating charges – rank in order of creation, ie oldest charges first.

Preferential debts in section 285, CA 1963 are:

– all local rates within the last twelve months
– all assessed taxes not exceeding one year's assessment
– all PRSI in the last year
– all wages or salary within the last four months
– all accrued holiday pay.

In a more complicated case, the following may also be used to decide the priorities of charges:

1. Fixed charges take priority over floating charges created over the same asset.
2. Legal charges take priority over equitable charges.
3. Floating charges rank in the order in which they were created, but a charge over a specific class of assets takes priority over an earlier charge over all the assets.
4. A company cannot create a second floating charge on the same assets ranking in priority to or equally with an existing floating charge.
5. A negative pledge clause is only valid if the holder of the subsequent charge has actual notice of the restriction.
6. A floating charge may be invalid under section 288, CA 1963 if it was registered within twelve months of a liquidation (or two years if in favour of a connected person), and the company was not solvent at the date of its creation.
7. Any charge may be invalid under section 286, CA 1963 as a fraudulent preference, if created within six months of a liquidation (or two years if in favour of a connected person).

Negative Pledge Clause

A negative pledge clause is usually a feature of a floating charge. It is a restriction on the borrowing company creating subsequent charges ranking in priority to the current one. This is to avoid the fear that a floating charge would lose out to a later fixed charge. A negative pledge clause binds both parties and also any subsequent secured creditors, provided they have actual notice of the clause. A subsequent charge holder will generally be aware of the previous charge because of the requirement of registration, but may not be aware of the prohibition contained therein, because it is not one of the essential facts required for registration.

Welch v Bowmaker and the Bank of Ireland (1980) Ire.
A company gave Bowmaker a floating charge over their land containing a negative pledge clause. A month later the company gave the Bank of Ireland an equitable deposit of title deeds over the same property. The Bank of Ireland were aware of the earlier floating charge, but did not know the details of its terms. On liquidation, there was insufficient money to pay both debts. Bowmaker argued that the Bank of Ireland as subsequent chargeholders should have *constructive notice*

of the negative pledge clause in the prior floating charge, because such clauses were so common.

Held: *Actual notice* was required, thus the second charge took priority as it was a fixed charge.

Invalidity of Charges

The liquidator can avoid paying certain charges:

1. Floating Charge Invalid under Section 288, CA 1963

A floating charge may be invalid under section 288, CA 1963, as amended by section 136, CA 1990, if registered within twelve months of a liquidation, unless it is proved that the company was solvent immediately after the creation of the charge. If the floating charge was created in favour of a 'connected person' any floating charge within the last two years shall be void.

A 'connected person' means:

- a director of the company
- a shadow director of the company
- a director's spouse, parent, brother, sister, child
- a trustee of a trust, the principal beneficiaries of which are a director, their spouse or children or any company they control
- a partner under the Partnership Act 1890
- the sole member of a single member private limited company is a person connected with the director of that company (unless the contrary is shown).

Solvent for the purposes of section 288 means 'an ability to pay its debts as they fall due'.

2. Fraudulent Preference Under Section 286, CA 1963

Section 286, CA 1963, as amended by section 135, CA 1990, provides that any act relating to property done by a company which is unable to pay its debts, in favour of a creditor, with a view to giving such creditor a preference over other creditors, shall be invalid if created within six months of a liquidation.

In other words, where a company is in financial difficulty and does something in an attempt to fraudulently prefer one creditor over another, this will be invalid. Typically, where a company has a number of unsecured creditors, it might create a floating charge in favour of one creditor, with the result that they are in a favourable position when the company is wound up. However, such a transaction will not be valid if it is within six months of the company being wound up, or two years if in favour of a connected person. (See chapter 18.)

10

RECEIVERSHIP

Receiverships

The appointment of a receiver is the remedy open to a debenture holder whose debt has fallen into arrears. The function of a receiver is to go into a company, sell off the charged assets and pay off the principal and interest due on debentures.

Qualifications and Disqualifications

A receiver is usually an accountant. Section 315, CA 1963, as amended by section 170, CA 1990 disqualifies the following from being receivers:

– a company
– an undischarged bankrupt
– a person who has been an officer or servant of the company within the last twelve months
– the partner or employee of an officer
– a spouse, parent, brother, sister or child of an officer.

Appointment

A receiver may be appointed by the terms of the debenture or debenture trust deed for reasons stated, or by the Court, if

– the principal or interest is in arrears
– the company has begun to be wound up
– the security is in jeopardy.

The appointment must be notified to the Registrar, the company, and the public.

Effect of Appointment

The effect of appointment is that:

1. floating charges crystallise
2. directors cannot make management decisions in relation to the charged asset

3. contracts of employment: the effect of the appointment of a receiver on the employees' contracts of employment varies depending on whom the receiver is said to be the agent of:

   – if the receiver is the agent of the debenture holder – employees are automatically dismissed
   – if the receiver is the agent/officer of the court – employees are automatically dismissed
   – if the receiver is the agent of the company – employees are *not* automatically dismissed

4. a receiver can sell the charged asset for the best price obtainable in the circumstances under section 316A, CA 1963 as inserted by section 172, CA 1990.

Ruby Property Company Ltd v Kilty (1999) Ire.
A receiver sold company property on the advice of an estate agent but without advertising it publicly.
Held: A receiver may have a duty to consider representations from the company as to how to conduct a sale to comply with section 318A, CA 1963.

5. a receiver is not liable on contracts made by the company prior to his/her appointment.

However, a receiver may be compelled to pay on such a contract through court action by the creditor.

W & L Crowe Ltd v ESB (1984) Ire.
The ESB refused to supply power to the receiver until the company's debts were settled. The receiver sought the advice of the High Court on whether to pay the account.
Held: The ESB were entitled to refuse to enter into a new supply contract with the receiver until the company's account was paid.

The receiver will be personally liable on any new contracts which he or she enters into, under section 316, CA 1963. However, the terms of a receiver's appointment will normally indemnify or insure the receiver against liability in the performance of his or her functions, except in the case of negligence.

Conduct of a Receivership

A 'statement of affairs' must be given to the receiver within fourteen days of his or her appointment, by the directors and secretary of the company, detailing the company's assets and liabilities, creditors and security. Within two months of appointment, the receiver must give a copy of the statement of affairs to the Registrar and the company, with comments relating to the course of the receivership.

A receiver may be removed if there are good grounds to do so, and another receiver appointed under section 175, CA 1990. A receiver is often removed and replaced with a liquidator under section 176, CA 1990 if the company goes into liquidation after the receiver has been appointed.

Receiver's Duties

1. The receiver and debenture holder have a fiduciary relationship, ie the receiver must act in the best interests of the debenture holder (regardless of whose agent the receiver is said to be, or the method of appointment).
2. The receiver's main duty to the company is to get the best price available in the circumstances for the sale of the charged asset, under section 316A, CA 1963 as inserted by section 172, CA 1990. Pre-1990 cases indicate that the test which the courts would probably apply to the receiver's decisions is one of reasonableness.
3. The receiver is under a duty of skill and care, and may be liable in negligence to the debenture holder and the company. Section 316, CA 1963 provides that a receiver will be personally liable on contracts unless the contract specifically provides otherwise.
4. The receiver has a duty to report to the company, via the statement of affairs.
5. The receiver may apply to the High Court for directions in relation to any matter connected with the performance of his/her duties as receiver under section 316, CA 1963. (This option is also open to any officer, member, employee or creditor of the company.)
6. The receiver must comply with any request from the Director of Corporate Enforcement to produce the receiver's books for examination.
7. The receiver must pay the company's debts in the correct order. This is known as the application of assets:

   – the costs of the receivership
   – the fixed charges in the order in which they were created
   – the preferential debts (*pari passu* or equally)
   – the floating charges in the order in which they were created
   – the unsecured creditors.

As a receivership often leads to a liquidation, a receiver may be removed by the High Court where a liquidator has also been appointed. This avoids extra expense and duplication of tasks.

11

DIRECTORS

A director is usually defined as a person involved in the management of a company.

Every company must have at least two directors, under section 174, CA 1963. Section 43 of the Companies (Amendment) (No. 2) Act 1999 requires that at least one of a company's directors shall be resident in the State, but since the Companies (Auditing and Accounting) Act 2003, this section does not apply to an alternate director. (There is an exception for a company which provides a bond of €25,400 which can be called upon if the company fails to pay a fine imposed under the Companies Acts 1963–2003 and the Taxes Consolidation Act 1997.)

Section 45, C(A)A (No. 2) 1999 provides that a person shall not be a director of more than twenty-five companies at any one time.

Types of directors

There are a number of different types of directors:

Executive and Non-Executive

An executive director is someone who manages the company on a full-time basis. A non-executive director is someone who manages the company on a part-time basis.

Managing Director

A managing director is the person to whom the board of directors has delegated power to carry on the day-to-day management of the company. The MD is the agent of the company.

Director for Life

A director for life is a position exclusive to a private company and is normally a reward for an entrepreneur.

Alternate Director

An alternate director is a substitute director who can attend and vote at meetings when another director cannot. A fellow director may be appointed as an alternate, or an outsider may be appointed. Such an appointment may be revoked by the board or the company in general meeting.

Shadow Director

According to section 27, CA 1990 a shadow director is someone in accordance with whose instructions the directors act. This person will be liable as a director in cases such as fraudulent trading. A professional advisor will not be treated as a shadow director.

Re Vehicle Imports Ltd (2001) Ire.
Held: A company accountant was liable as a shadow director where he overstepped his role, as evidenced by his being given excessive salary payments and blank cheques.

Re Gasco Ltd (2001) Ire.
Held: A fifty per cent shareholder who effectively ran the company after the resignation of its two directors was held to be a shadow director.

Appointment of Directors

Under section 181, CA 1963 directors may only be appointed individually. The procedure for appointment is in the articles of association. Section 178, CA 1963 provides that the acts of a director shall be valid, notwithstanding any defect which may afterwards be discovered in their appointment or qualification.

Retirement

Retirement of directors is 'by rotation', under Article 92 of Table A. Each year, one third of the directors (or the nearest number) must offer to resign. This provision does not apply to the managing director or a director for life in a private company.

Resignation

A director may resign by giving notice in writing to the company.
    A casual vacancy is a vacancy which arises between annual general meetings, due perhaps to death or resignation. A casual vacancy may

be filled by the remaining directors co-opting a person on to the board, until the next election.

Removal

A director may be removed from a company by an ordinary resolution according to section 182, CA 1963. Extended notice of twenty-eight days is required in respect of any such resolution. In theory, a director for life in a private company cannot be removed. However, it is possible to remove a director for life in certain circumstances where they have breached their duties to the company (see *Shuttleworth v Cox Bros (Maidenhead) Ltd* (1927), chapter 4). If the director for life is named as such in the articles of association, he or she can only be removed by a special resolution altering the article in question.

Compensation for Removal

Section 182(7), CA 1963 provides that a removed director may however have the right to damages for breach of contract for wrongful dismissal, or for unfair dismissal if he/she was an employee. Companies must also observe the requirements of natural justice, and fairness, in the removal of directors.

Glover v BLN Ltd (1973) Ire.
Held: There had been a breach of natural justice in the failure to give reasons for removal, thus Glover was entitled to damages for wrongful dismissal.

Carville v Irish Industrial Bank (1968) Ire.
Held: No notice had been given of removal, thus damages for wrongful dismissal were awarded.

Section 28, CA 1990 limits directors' service contracts to a maximum of five years. This is to avoid companies paying 'golden parachutes' on removal of directors.

Ineligibility

The 1963 Companies Act prohibits the following people from acting as directors:

- undischarged bankrupts
- a body corporate
- the auditor of the company or its holding company.

Disqualification

Section 159, CA 1990 defines disqualification as disqualification from acting as an auditor, director, officer, receiver, liquidator, examiner in relation to any company, and from taking part in the direct or indirect promotion, formation or management of any company. The articles of association can provide for disqualification of certain directors, and the High Court can do so as well.

Disqualification under the Articles

Table A, Article 39 usually provides that directors must vacate their office:

1. if they fail to acquire their share qualifications, as required by section 180, CA 1963
2. if they become bankrupt or make an arrangement with their creditors
3. if they become prohibited from being a director by reason of any order made by the High Court under Part VII, CA 1990 in relation to disqualification and restriction of directors
4. if they become of unsound mind
5. if they resign their office by notice in writing to the company
6. if they are convicted of any indictable offence (other directors may waive this)
7. if they have been absent without leave from board meetings for more than six months.
8. if they are directly or indirectly interested in a contract with the company and fail to declare it under section 194, CA 1963.

Disqualification by Court

Under section 160, CA 1990, the following people are automatically disqualified from acting as directors:

1. a person convicted of an indictable offence relating to the company or an offence involving fraud or dishonesty while acting as director, promoter, officer, auditor, receiver, liquidator or examiner of a company.
2. a person who has been guilty of fraud while in the roles mentioned in 1. above.
3. a person guilty of reckless or fraudulent trading
4. a person unfit to be involved in the management of a company, by reason of his conduct in the roles mentioned in 1. above

5. a person unfit to be involved in the management of a company following an inspector's report under the Companies Acts, by reason of their conduct in the roles mentioned in 1. above
6. a person persistently in default in relation to the filing requirements of the Companies Acts
7. a person convicted of acting as promoter, officer, auditor, receiver, liquidator or examiner of a company, while an undischarged bankrupt under section 169, CA 1990.

The High Court also has discretion to disqualify in other cases.

An application for a disqualification order can be made by the Director of Public Prosecutions, the Registrar of Companies or the Director of Corporate Enforcement. Section 56 of the CLEA 2001 provides that a liquidator of an insolvent company must apply to the court to restrict the directors under section 150, CA 1990. A disqualification order must be notified to the Registrar of Companies, who keeps a register of persons disqualified under s168 CA 1990.

If the court judges that disqualification is not justified, it may make a restriction order under section 150, CA 1990.

Restriction

Section 150, CA 1990 (as amended by section 41, of the Company Law Enforcement Act 2001) restricts a director of an insolvent company from being a director of another company for five years. This is to avoid an abuse of the concept of separate legal personality by what is known as 'phoenix trading'.

Under section 150, a person who was a director, including a shadow director, of a company within twelve months of it going into insolvent liquidation, will be restricted for a period of five years from acting as a director or secretary or from taking part in the promotion or the formation of another company. A High Court application for restriction of a director under section 150 may be made by a receiver, a liquidator or the Director of Corporate Enforcement. The court may order a director to bear the cost of such an application. When the court makes a restriction order, it must notify the Registrar of Companies, who keeps a register of persons restricted, under s153 CA 1990.

However, the legislation does provide for a number of limited exceptions to this restriction:

1. if the director acted honestly and responsibly and there is no other reason why it would be just and equitable to restrict him or her

2. if he/she was a director solely as nominee of a financial institution lending to the company, and that institution has not obtained any personal guarantee of repayment from a director
3. if he/she was a director solely as a nominee of a venture capital company.

Both 2. and 3. are also subject to the requirement that they must have acted honestly and responsibly.

Re Streamline Ltd (1998) Ire., held that the burden of proof is on the directors to show that they acted honestly and responsibly.

Business Communications Ltd v Baxter and Parsons (1995) Ire.
Held: acting 'responsibly' entails compliance with the Companies Acts and maintenance of records required by the Companies Acts.

A restricted director may act for a highly capitalised company, that is one which has an allotted share capital of at least €63,500 in a private company and €317,500 in a public company, fully paid up in cash. If such a company takes on a restricted director, it loses the benefit of certain provisions on capital maintenance.

If a restricted director acts as director of another company which goes into liquidation within twelve months, the restricted director can be made personally liable without limit for the debts of the second company.

It is a criminal offence to act for a company while restricted and this leads to automatic disqualification. Relief from restriction can be sought under section 152, CA 1990. A director may apply to the court within one year of restriction, for relief, and the court may grant relief as it sees fit.

Business Communications Ltd v Baxter and Parsons (1995) Ire.
A company traded for six months while insolvent before going into voluntary liquidation.
Held: The directors were restricted and not granted an exemption.

La Moselle Clothing Ltd v Soualhi (1998) Ire.
S was a director and 99 per cent shareholder of M Ltd. S was restricted because the company had traded while insolvent.
Held: The court established a test to determine whether a director is acting responsibly, i.e. the following must be considered:

1. the extent of compliance with the Companies Acts

2. whether the director's conduct was so incompetent as to be irresponsible
3. the extent of the director's responsibility for insolvency
4. the extent of the director's responsibility for the net deficiency in assets at winding up
5. the extent to which the director displayed a lack of commercial probity or want of proper standards.

This test was approved by the Supreme Court in *Re Squash (Ireland) Ltd* (2001) Ire.

Re Dunlecky Ltd (1999) Ire.
Held: A director's failure to file a statutory statement of affairs during the company's liquidation was grounds to impose a restriction order.

Re Gasco Ltd (2001) Ire.
Held: A shadow director was restricted after a liquidator found no books or records in the company. By contrast, two other directors who had acted honestly and responsibly were not.

Re Vehicle Imports Ltd (2001) Ire.
Held: A company accountant was held to be a shadow director and was restricted following liquidation of the company.

Directors' Duties

Article 80 of Table A states 'the business of the company shall be managed by the directors' and the directors 'may exercise all such powers of the company as are not, by the Companies Acts, required to be exercised by the company in general meeting'. Directors' duties are owed by all types of directors, regardless of their level of involvement or payment, as stated in *Re Costello Doors Ltd* (1995) Ire. and *Re Vehicle Imports Ltd* (2001) Ire.

Directors owe three main duties to a company:

1. Fiduciary Duties

A fiduciary duty is a duty to act in the best interests of another person. The duty is owed to the shareholders at large. The following specific duties exist:

1. Directors must act in good faith in the best interests of the company as a whole.

Re Lee Behrens & Co (1932)
Held: A pension to the widow of a former director was of no benefit to the company.

Parke v Daily News (1961)
Held: A gift of €2 million to employees was not in the best interests of the company as a whole.

Crindle Investments v Wymes (1998) Ire.
Held: Directors do not, merely by virtue of their office, owe a fiduciary duty to individual shareholders, although they may do so in exceptional circumstances. Directors' duties are owed to the company as a whole.

It is arguable that case law such as *Re Frederick Inns* (1994) Ire., *Re Streamline Ltd* (1998) Ire. and *La Moselle Clothing Ltd* (1998) Ire. has extended this directors' duty to creditors, but this has not yet been clearly established.

Under section 52, CA 1990 directors of a company must have regard to the interests of the employees, as well as the members, in the performance of their duties.

2. Directors must exercise their powers for the purposes for which they were conferred. If there is more than one purpose the courts look at the 'substantial purpose'.

   – Illegal acts: directors may be liable to the company for such. Illegal acts cannot be ratified by a company, even unanimously, but shareholders can absolve directors from liability to compensate the company.
   – Ultra vires acts: cannot be ratified by shareholders. Section 8, CA 1963 allows third parties to enforce such acts. Shareholders can seek to stop them by injunction (see chapter 4).
   – Difficulties may arise where directors allot new shares in the company to themselves. (This is now subject to C(A)A 1983 whereby directors must get prior approval from shareholders for allotment of new shares (see chapter 5).)

Nash v Lancegaye (Ireland) Safety Glass Ltd and Another (1958) Ire.
R held 49 per cent of the votes. The remaining votes were held by Nash and proxies. Following differences, R allotted more shares to increase his vote to 51 per cent.
Held: The main reason was to dilute the plaintiff to a minority and this was not in the best interest of the company as a whole. The

allotment was therefore ineffective (and possibly oppression under section 205, CA 1963).

Howard Smith Ltd v Ampol Petroleum Ltd (1974)

Two director-shareholders held 55 per cent of the shares in a company between them and honestly supported a forthcoming take-over bid for the company. They allotted new shares to the take-over bidder so that the bid would succeed.

Held: The directors' power to allot shares was used for an improper purpose, i.e. to dilute the power of the minority.

- In a private company directors usually have discretion to refuse to register a transfer of existing shares to a new shareholder. Difficulties arise where they refuse to transfer:

Re Hafner Olhausen v Powderly (1943) Ire.

Directors had 'absolute and uncontrolled' discretion to refuse transfer without giving reasons. These directors did so, and the decision was challenged.

Held: The directors could refuse but the court could draw inferences of improper purpose from the refusal.

3. Directors must avoid any conflict of interest. A conflict usually takes one of two forms:

(a) Diverting Business Opportunity from the Company

Cooke v Deeks (1916)

Three directors negotiated a contract on behalf of a company, then took the contract for themselves.

Held: They were accountable for the profit.

Industrial Development Consultants Ltd v Cooley (1972)

The MD negotiated a lucrative contract for IDC, but the bid was rejected. The MD feigned illness to get out of his employment in order to take on the contract personally.

Held: This was a conflict of interest and breach of duty. The profits he made were found to be held on 'constructive trust' for the plaintiff company.

Section 194, CA 1963 now requires directors to disclose their interest in contracts made by the company. The disclosure should be made at the meeting which considers the contract, or at the first meeting after the director becomes interested. Disclosure to part of the board is insufficient (*Guinness plc v Saunders and Ward* (1988)). A conflict of interest register must be kept.

(b) Interest in Another Business/Secret Profit

An interest in a competing company is not of itself a conflict of interest, but may be limited by a director's service contract. Most of the cases below could have been avoided by disclosure by the directors.

Aberdeen Railway Co v Blaikie Bros (1854)
BB contracted to supply goods to ARC. The MD of ARC was also a managing partner in BB.
Held: The purchase contract was voidable at the option of ARC.

Regal Hastings v Gulliver (1942)
Directors made substantial profit on the sale of a subsidiary.
Held: The directors were liable to account for profits, although they acted in good faith and there was no loss to the company.

2. *Duty of Skill and Care*

Directors owe a duty of care to the company to exercise all due skill and care. The standard of care owed has been established in *Re City Equitable Ltd.* (1925) which established three principles:

1. The duty of skill and care is a subjective test, based on the knowledge and experience of the particular director.
2. Directors can delegate or leave the routine business of the company to the management, provided it is normal business practice and there are no suspicious circumstances which should put the directors on notice to look further into the issue.
3. A director's duty of care to the company is owed at board meetings only. In addition, a director need only attend board meetings 'regularly'.

Cases on directors' negligence are relatively rare:

Dorchester Finance Ltd v Stebbings (1977)
The defendants were three directors of the plaintiff company. S and P were chartered accountants; H had much business experience. S and P were non-executive directors who rarely visited the company and signed blank cheques for H. H mismanaged the company and the company claimed against all three in negligence.

Held:
- A director must use a degree of skill as reasonably expected from a person with his knowledge and experience.
- A director should take such care in the performance of his duties as an ordinary person might take on his own behalf.
- A director must exercise his powers honestly, in good faith and in the best interests of the company – *Re City Equitable.*

The directors were liable. The standard of care was judged from their professional experience and qualifications.

La Moselle Clothing Ltd (1998) Ire.
While a case of restriction and not an action for negligence, this case gives five tests of when a director is acting responsibly.

CMS Dolphin Ltd v Simonet (2001)
The MD of a PR company resigned and set up his own business. All the staff of the company and most of the clients joined the new business.
Held: A director is liable for profits made where he expropriated a business opportunity, regardless of whether this was done personally or through a company.

Release of Directors from Liability

Section 200, CA 1963, as amended by section 56 Companies (Auditing and Accounting) Act 2003, provides that any provision in the articles of a company which exempt any officer, or auditor, of a company from liability arising out of any negligence, default, breach of duty or breach of trust shall be void. However, a company may purchase and maintain liability insurance for any of its officers or auditors. A director may be part of a quorum and vote upon a resolution to purchase liability insurance under which the director might benefit. (A company may also indemnify any officer or auditor from liability in defending proceedings in which judgment is given in his or her favour or in which he or she is acquitted).

There are very few decided cases of directors breaching their common law duties, which suggests that the duty of skill and care is low, and that these duties are in fact easily fulfilled. This has led to an increase in directors' statutory duties since 1990.

3. Statutory Duties

The Companies Act 1990 requires directors to disclose certain transactions and prohibits others. This is intended to make directors more accountable for their actions.

(a) Loans to Directors

Section 31, CA 1990 now prohibits a company from making loans to its directors, ie:

- making a loan or quasi-loan to a director of a company or its holding company
- making a loan or quasi-loan to a person connected with a director
- entering into a credit transaction as creditor for a director or connected person
- entering into a guarantee or providing security for a loan, quasi-loan or credit transaction made by a director or connected person.

A 'connected person' (under section 26, CA 1990) is:

- spouse, parent, brother, sister or child of a director
- a partner under the Partnership Act 1890
- the trustee of a trust which benefits a director, his or her children or any company he or she controls.
- the sole member of a single member private limited company is a person connected with the director of that company (unless the contrary is shown).

There are exceptions to the ban on loans in the 1990 Act. Under section 32, CA 1990, a company may loan money to its directors or connected persons if the loan is:

- less than ten per cent of the value of the company's assets
- the advancing of money to a director for reasonable expenses.

The penalties for breach of section 31 are:

- The director or connected person must account to the company for any gains made as a result of the transaction.
- The prohibited transaction is voidable at the company's option.
- If the company is subsequently wound up and the court considers that a transaction prohibited by section 31 'contributed materially' to its insolvency, or 'substantially impeded the orderly winding up' of the company, the court may declare any person who benefited from such a prohibited loan to be personally liable for the company's debts, with or without limit.

The Company Law Enforcement Act 2001 introduced new rules for companies guaranteeing or securing loans by another person to the director, or connected person, of a holding company. The company must approve the guarantee by special resolution and statutory declaration.

(b) Substantial Property Transactions Involving Directors

Section 29, CA 1990 provides:

- where a director or connected person is to acquire a non-cash asset from the company, or
- where the company is to acquire a non-cash asset from a director or connected person
- and the value of the asset exceeds €63,500 or ten percent of the company's assets

the transaction must first be approved by a resolution in a general meeting.

There are similar provisions to enforce these requirements in that the director or connected person must account to the company for any gain. However, breach of section 29 is not a criminal offence.

(c) Directors' Interests in Shares

Section 30, CA 1990 prohibits directors buying options to buy or sell shares of the company or its associated companies.

Section 53, CA 1990 provides that directors must also disclose their dealings or interests in shares or debentures in the company or its associated companies.

(d) Political Donations by Companies

Section 26 of the Electoral Act 1997 requires that donations for political purposes exceeding €5,079 must be included in the Director's Report under section 158, CA 1963 and in the Annual Report under sections 125 and 126, CA 1963. A donation is any money, property, or goods supplied at less than commercial rates, any use of property or goods without payment, or supply of services without payment, for members or candidates for the Dáil, Seanad, or European Parliament.

(e) Directors' Compliance Statements

This statutory duty under section 45 of the Companies (Auditing and Accounting) Act 2003 imposes an obligation on the directors of certain companies to prepare a Compliance Policy Statement and an

Annual Compliance Statement for inclusion in the Directors' Report that accompanies the company's audited financial statements. This only applies to a minority of companies, i.e.

– all public limited companies (whether listed or not), and
– all private companies whose turnover exceeds €15.23 million or whose balance sheet total exceeds €7.6 million.

The Directors' Compliance Statements will report on compliance with the company's 'relevant obligations'. This covers the Companies Acts, tax law and any other legal framework within which the company operates and that may materially affect the company's financial statements.

There are two compliance statements. The Compliance Policy Statement looks forward to identify what policies, arrangements and procedures are in place to secure the company's compliance with its present and future relevant obligations. In contrast, the Annual Compliance Statement looks back to report on the company's compliance with its relevant obligations in the preceding financial year.

Personal Liability of Directors

A director can be declared to be personally liable for the debts of the company:

1. where the corporate veil is lifted
2. where a company is unlimited
3. where there is fraudulent trading under section 297, CA 1963 as inserted by section 137, CA 1990
4. where there is reckless trading under section 297A, CA 1963 as inserted by section 138, CA 1990
5. where a director has made a false declaration of solvency in a voluntary member's liquidation
6. where a director has made a false declaration of solvency when a company gave financial assistance for the purchase of the company's shares
7. where a director acts while restricted
8. where any officer acts on the instructions of a restricted director
9. where the company failed to keep proper books of account, which contributed to the company going into insolvent liquidation
10. where the company made a prohibited loan to a director which materially contributed to the company going into insolvent liquidation

11. where a director was disqualified and the company was liqui-
    dated within twelve months of the disqualification.

A shadow director can be made liable for acting in any of the above
circumstances.

Legal Action Against Directors

Section 55 of the Company Law Enforcement Act 2001 provides that
the High Court may order a director or other officer not to remove
his or her assets outside the jurisdiction. The company, a director,
member, receiver, liquidator, creditor or the Director of Corporate
Enforcement may apply, and the court may make the order where it is
satisfied that

- the applicant has a substantive civil action or claim for damages,
  and
- there are grounds for believing that the respondent may remove or
  dispose of his or her or the company's assets with a view to
  frustrating a court order.

Company Officers

Where reference is made to the 'officers of a company', this includes
a director or secretary, according to section 2, CA 1963.

12

THE COMPANY SECRETARY AND AUDITOR

Every company must have a secretary according to section 175, CA 1963. The secretary may also be one of the directors. A company secretary can be a body corporate.

Appointment of the Company Secretary

The first company secretary may be named in the memorandum or articles of association.

Qualification

Section 236, CA 1990 declares that the directors of a public company must ensure that the secretary of the company has the necessary knowledge and experience. They must ensure that the secretary is qualified, ie:

– was a secretary of the company at the commencement of the section
– was a secretary of a company for three out of the five years prior to their appointment
– is a person who appears to the directors to be capable of discharging the functions, based on their experience or professional membership
– is a member of a relevant professional body recognised by the Minister for Enterprise, Trade and Employment.

There are no qualifications for a secretary of a private company.

Duties

A secretary's duties are not defined in legislation. The duties are administrative and not managerial. A secretary's duties are to ensure that the company complies with the Companies Acts. The specific duties are as follows:

- to keep charge of the statutory registers
- to make the annual return to the Registrar of Companies
- to give members due notice of meetings
- to keep minutes of general meetings and board meetings
- to file details of all charges with the Registrar of Companies.

A secretary is often the chief administrative officer of a company, and thus has power to bind the company as agent in day-to-day contracts. This is the usual authority of a secretary as agent.

A secretary may be given express authority to act on behalf of a company. He or she may also have implied authority to act as company agent in respect of administrative contracts, ie the secretary may have usual authority to act as agent and also apparent authority.

Panorama Developments Ltd v Fidelis Furnishing Ltd (1971)
Held: A secretary had apparent authority to make contracts to hire cars. This decision recognises that the secretary can have wide general duties.

Company officers: Where reference is made to the 'officers of a company', this includes a director or secretary, according to section 2, CA 1963.

The Auditor

Under section 160, CA 1963, every company must appoint an auditor at a general meeting. However, this rule was modified by section 32, C(A)(no.2)A 1999 as amended by section 53, C(A&A)A 2003 which allows for the removal of the statutory audit for small companies. If a private company's turnover does not exceed €1.5 million, the balance sheet total does not exceed €1.9 million and the average number of employees does not exceed 50, the directors can decide to avail of the exemption from having accounts audited (see chapter 3).

Companies which do not avail of section 32, C(A)(No.2)A 1999 must get an auditor to analyse the annual accounts and ensure that they give a true and fair account of the company's affairs. An auditor must be suitably qualified, registered and independent, and must not have been disqualified. The Companies (Auditing and Accounting) Act 2003 amended the rules from the original CA 1990.

Qualifications of an Auditor

Section 187, CA 1990 as amended by section 35, C(A&A)A 2003 sets out the acceptable categories of person or firm qualified to act as an auditor, which are:

1. members of the following recognised accounting bodies: ACA, ACCA, IIPA
2. persons training with any of the recognised accounting bodies
3. persons authorised by the Minister to be practising members of accountancy bodies recognised under the Companies Act 1963 and under the law of another country.
4. a firm shall be qualified to act as an auditor if at least one member is entitled to hold a practising certificate from a recognised accountancy body.

Section 72 of the Company Law Enforcement Act 2001 amends section 187, CA 1990 by providing that the Director may demand that a purported auditor produce evidence of his or her qualifications. Failure to do so is an offence.

Registered Auditor

A qualified auditor must also be registered with the Registrar of Companies under section 198, CA 1990 as amended by section 38, C(A&A)A 2003.

The following are disqualified from acting as an auditor under section 187, CA 1990:

1. an officer or servant of the company
2. an ex-officer or ex-servant of the company, within a period in respect of which accounts would be audited by them if they were appointed auditor
3. a parent, spouse, brother, sister or child of an officer of the company
4. a partner or employee of an officer of the company
5. a person who is disqualified from being an auditor of the company's holding company or subsidiary
6. a body corporate.

Appointment and Re-appointment

The first auditor of a company may be appointed by the directors before the first AGM, according to section 160, CA 1963, and holds office until that meeting.

Section 160, as amended by section 183, CA 1990 provides that a retiring auditor will be re-appointed without any resolution being passed unless:

- the auditor is not qualified for reappointment
- the auditor does not wish to be reappointed
- a resolution has been passed to appoint another person as auditor.

Under section 35, C(A)(No. 2) Act 1999 a company must appoint an auditor as soon as possible after it becomes clear that any of the conditions necessary for availing of the exemption from an audit no longer apply.

Removal

An auditor may be removed from office by an ordinary resolution requiring extended notice of twenty-eight days, under section 183, CA 1990. An auditor who is being removed may contact the company and shareholders and attend the relevant AGM. Under section 34, C(A) (No. 2) Act 1999 a company may discontinue the appointment of an auditor where it avails of the exemption from the statutory audit. The auditor must serve notice on the company that there are no circumstances which affect the exemption, or state such circumstances if they exist.

Retirement

Under section 185, CA 1990 an auditor can resign during his or her term of office. If there are circumstances to be brought to the attention of the members or creditors, the company must do so, or the auditor may call a general meeting to consider the issue.

Auditor's Powers and Duties

Under section 193, CA 1990 an auditor has power to access all written information and ask questions of the company's employees and officers.

(a) Duty to Report to Members

Section 193, CA 1990 states that the auditor shall report to the members on the accounts examined by them, and on every balance sheet, profit and loss account and all group accounts laid before the company in general meeting during his/her term of office. The auditor must state that in his or her opinion, the accounts reflect the company's true financial position. If the auditor believes that the company has failed to keep proper books of account, the auditor shall notify the company and the Registrar, who in turn will notify the Director of Corporate Enforcement.

Under section 45 of C(A&A)A 2003 directors of certain large companies must prepare a Compliance Policy Statement and an

Annual Compliance Statement for inclusion in the Directors' Report that accompanies the company's audited financial statements (see chapter 11). In such companies, the auditors must review the Directors' Compliance Statements to determine if they are 'fair and reasonable'.

(b) Duty to Investigate and Report

The duty to investigate and report was expressed in *Re Kingston Cotton Mill Co (No. 2) (1896)*, as a duty to be 'a watchdog and not a bloodhound'.

An auditor's report must state that all the necessary information has been obtained, and that in the auditor's opinion, proper books of account were kept, proper returns were received, and the balance sheet and profit and loss account are in agreement with the accounts and returns. Overall, the accounts must give the information required by the Companies Acts, and give a true and fair view. An auditor must give a qualified opinion if there are circumstances which require information to be drawn to the attention of the company.

(c) Duty to Act with Professional Integrity

Section 193, CA 1990 states that an auditor shall be under a general duty to carry out the audit with professional integrity.

(d) Duty of Skill and Care

If an auditor fails to perform his or her duties with reasonable skill and care, he or she may be liable to the company. An auditor has:

– a duty to the company in contract
– a potential duty to third parties in tort.

Hedley Byrne & Co Ltd v Heller & Partners Ltd (1964)
Held: Established the principle of legal liability for a negligent mis-statement by a person who gives information to another, knowing that the information is going to be relied on.

This set a precedent that auditors could be liable to persons with whom they had a 'special relationship', and thus could foresee that the other person would rely on the annual accounts which they had audited.

However, this precedent has been changed in England.

Caparo Industries plc v Touche Ross (1990)
Held: An audit is done to comply with the Companies Acts, not to provide information to the public or potential investors. Thus an

auditor did not owe a duty of care to potential take-over bidders, as the auditor did not know that the information was going to be relied on for such a purpose.

Also held: The auditors had no liability to existing shareholders on an individual basis, but only as a group.

(e) The Finance Act 1995

The Finance Act 1995 imposes duties on an auditor in relation to the commission of certain tax offences.

Section 172 of the Finance Act 1995 provides that where an auditor of a company becomes aware that a company has committed or is committing an offence in relation to taxation, they shall

- communicate the offence to the company, and
- request the company to take action to rectify the matter or notify an officer of the Revenue Commissioners.

Unless the auditor is satisfied that the company has done this, the auditor shall cease to act as auditor for three years, or until they are satisfied that the necessary notification of the offence has taken place.

Section 194(4), CA 1990 as inserted by section 74, CLEA 2001 provides that where an auditor comes to the opinion that a company or its officers or agents have committed an indictable offence under the Companies Acts, it shall notify the Director of Corporate Enforcement providing details. Compliance with this section is not regarded as a contravention of an auditor's professional or legal duties.

Section 37, C(A&A)A 2003 amended section 194, CA 1990 to provide that when a company's auditors notify the Director, they shall, if requested by the Director,

- furnish the Director with such further information in their control or possession as required
- give the Director access to books and documents in their control or possession as required, and access to copies or extracts thereof.

This section does not compel disclosure of any information subject to legal professional privilege.

Irish Auditing and Accounting Supervisory Authority

The IAASA was created by the Companies (Auditing and Accounting) Act 2003, to supervise the regulatory functions of the recognised accountancy bodies. The main objectives of the authority under section 8 are:

- to supervise how the prescribed accountancy bodies regulate and monitor their members
- to promote adherence to high professional standards in the auditing and accountancy profession
- to monitor whether the accounts of certain classes of companies and other undertakings comply with the Companies Acts, and
- to act as a specialist source of advice to the Minister on auditing and accounting matters.

Its website is at www.iaasa.ie.

13

COMPANY MEETINGS

Company Meetings

Shareholders have the right to attend and vote at general meetings. The rights of different classes of shareholders are dealt with in chapter 6.

One Person Companies

Since the EC (Single Member Private Limited Companies) Regulations 1994 a company can be formed with only one shareholder. Section 8 of the 1994 regulations enables the sole member to dispense with the holding of an AGM, and if they do so section 131, CA 1963 shall not apply. The requirements of laying accounts and reports before a general meeting are satisfied where such information is sent to the single member.

However, an auditor may not be removed without calling the meeting as required by section 160, CA 1963. A quorum is a single member present in person or by proxy, under section 10 of the 1994 Regulations.

Annual General Meeting

In circumstances other than a single member company, section 131, CA 1963 applies.

A company must hold an AGM every calendar year. The maximum time allowed between AGMs is fifteen months. However, if the first AGM takes place within eighteen months of incorporation, there need not be another general meeting in the first two years. A company's AGM must be held in the State, unless the articles provide otherwise (section 140, CA 1963).

If the company directors fail to call an AGM, under section 131, CA 1963, any member may apply to the Director of Corporate Enforcement to call the meeting. A company may be prosecuted for failure to hold an AGM, as in *Re Muckross Park Hotel Ltd* (2001) Ire.

Notice

By section 133, CA 1963, twenty-one days notice in writing must be given of the AGM, giving the time, the place and the issues to be considered. Section 133 also provides that 'short notice' can be given if all the shareholders entitled to attend and vote, and the company's auditors agree.

The main business of an AGM is consideration of the profit and loss account, the balance sheet, the auditor's report and the directors' report.

The ordinary business to be conducted at an AGM is as follows:

- the declaration of a dividend
- the consideration of the accounts
- the election of directors
- the re-appointment of the auditors (where a company has an auditor).

Special business is anything else, and appropriate notice must be given.

Extraordinary General Meeting

An extraordinary general meeting is any meeting which is not an AGM.
An EGM may be convened as follows:

1. Article 50, Table A provides that an EGM may be convened by the company directors as they think fit.
2. Section 132, CA 1963 states that the directors shall call an EGM, on the request of 10 per cent of the shareholders. If the directors fail to call such a meeting within twenty-one days, the shareholders themselves may convene a meeting, within three months.
3. Section 135, CA 1963 states that the High Court may order a meeting to be called and conducted as the court sees fit, or on the application of any director, or any member.
4. Other specific instances of general meetings:

   - Section 40, C(A)A 1983 provides that if the value of the net assets falls below half of the value of the called-up share capital, the directors shall convene a general meeting to consider what measures to take.
   - Section 186, CA 1990 provides that a resigning auditor may call an explanatory general meeting.
   - Section 251, CA 1963 provides that a company may be wound up voluntarily after the members pass a special resolution at an EGM.

Notice

The *minimum* lengths of notice are as follows:

- An annual general meeting in a private or public company requires twenty-one days written notice, under section 133, CA 1963.
- An extraordinary general meeting in a public company requires fourteen days written notice, under section 133, CA 1963.
- An extraordinary general meeting in a private company requires seven days written notice, under section 133, CA 1963.
- If a special resolution is proposed, twenty-one days written notice must be given, regardless of the type of meeting, under section 141, CA 1963.
- If an ordinary resolution requiring extended notice is proposed, twenty-eight days notice must be given, under section 142, CA 1963.

Short Notice

Section 133, CA 1963 provides for the calling of a meeting by short notice, where consent is given by all voting members and the auditor. (In the case of a meeting to consider a special resolution, short notice can be given by shareholders holding 90 per cent of the votes.)

Notice Procedure

Article 51 Table A provides:

- All notice is 'clear', ie exclusive of the day of service and the day of the meeting.
- The notice shall specify the date, time, place and general nature of any special business
- The accidental failure to give notice, or the non-receipt of notice of a meeting by any person entitled does not invalidate the procedures at the meeting.

Resolutions

The decisions that a company makes at a meeting are known as resolutions.

Ordinary resolutions may be proposed in advance of or at a general meeting, and are passed by a simple majority of the votes cast. Some ordinary resolutions require extended notice of twenty-eight days, eg:

- to remove a director under section 182, CA 1963
- to remove an auditor under section 161, CA 1963.

A company must give notice of the extended notice resolutions at the same time and in the same way as it gives notice of the meeting which will consider the resolution.

Special Resolutions

Special resolutions must be proposed twenty-one days in advance and passed by a three-quarters majority. Less than twenty-one days notice may be given if not less than 90 per cent of the members entitled to attend and vote agree to do so, according to section 141, CA 1963.

Special resolutions are used for major changes in a company, including:

– changing a company name
– altering a company memorandum or articles
– altering a company objects clause
– reducing a company share capital
– re-registering a private company as a public company, or vice versa
– permitting an off-market purchase of a company's own shares
– winding up a company.

All special resolutions must be registered in the Companies Registration Office (as must some specified ordinary ones).

Amending a Resolution

An amendment to an ordinary resolution is allowed if it is within the scope of the notice. However, an amendment to the substance of a special resolution is not allowed, ie the special resolution voted upon must be the one circulated in advance of the meeting, except for minor changes of expression and style.

Proceedings at Meetings

A decision of a meeting is only binding if certain conditions apply:

1. the meeting has been properly convened by notice (considered above)
2. a chairperson presides
3. the requisite quorum is present, and
4. all proceedings including voting are properly conducted.

Chairperson

Section 134, CA 1963 provides that the members present at a meeting may appoint any member as chairperson, but a company's articles usually provide otherwise. Article 104 provides that the directors may elect a chairperson for their meetings, and Article 56 then provides that the chairperson of the board of directors shall preside as chairperson at every general meeting.

The chairperson's function is to ensure that the meeting is properly conducted.

Article 58 provides that the chairperson may adjourn a meeting with the consent of the meeting. The chairperson also has a common law power to adjourn a meeting if it becomes disorderly, as seen in *Byng v London Life Assurance Ltd* (1987). No business shall be conducted at the adjourned meeting except the unfinished business from the original meeting. If a meeting is adjourned for thirty days or more, notice must be given for the adjourned meeting, as would be done for an original meeting. If a meeting is improperly adjourned, the members may appoint a new chairperson and continue.

Quorum

If there is no quorum (or minimum attendance), there can be no meeting. Unless the articles provide otherwise, the quorum will be as follows:

- Private company – two members personally present, section 134, CA, 1963. However, Article 54, Table A provides that in a private company three members 'present in person' shall be the quorum.
- Public company – three members personally present, section 134, CA 1963
- Single member private company – one member present or by proxy, section 10, EC (Single Member Private Limited Companies) Regulations 1994

Article 55 of Table A provides that if a quorum is not present within half an hour of the time appointed for the meeting, the meeting shall be adjourned to the same time and place of the same day of the next week, or any such time and place as the directors may determine. If there is no quorum at the adjourned meeting, the members present shall constitute a quorum.

In some companies, the articles may provide that the quorum must only be present at the beginning of the meeting. As seen in *Re Hartley Baird* (1955) resolutions taken later in a meeting are still valid.

Proper Proceedings

There are two methods of voting at company meetings:

- Show of hands: Unless the articles provide otherwise, all issues at a meeting are to be decided in the first place by a show of hands. Article 63 provides that each person present and every proxy has one vote, but voting members cannot vote on proxies for another shareholder.

The chairperson counts the hands, and his or her declaration of the result is conclusive, unless it is fraudulent or obviously wrong.

- Poll: Section, 137 CA 1963 provides that a poll may be demanded after a show of hands. Each share carries one vote. A poll overrides a vote on a show of hands and is used for important issues. Under section 137, a poll can be demanded by either not less than five shareholders who have the right to vote, or shareholders holding 10 per cent of the voting rights.

Article 59, Table A further provides that a poll can be demanded by:

- the chairperson
- at least three members present in person or by proxy
- shareholders holding 10 per cent of the voting rights, in person or by proxy.

The right to a poll can be excluded when it concerns the election of a chairperson or the adjournment of a meeting.

Proxies

Section 136, CA 1963 provides that any member of a company entitled to attend and vote at a meeting shall be entitled to appoint another person to attend, speak and vote instead. Notice of the meeting must state this right. In a plc, 'two-way proxies' are often used. These enable members to include in the proxy form an instruction to vote for or against the proposals. In the absence of such a clause, proxies are given discretion on how to vote.

'Meeting' by Written Resolution

Section 141, CA 1963 provides that, if a company's articles allow it, a written resolution signed by all members entitled to attend and vote at a meeting, shall be valid and effective for all purposes, as if the resolution had been passed at a general meeting duly convened and held.

Meeting Irregularity

Common law provides that in the case of a private company, if a meeting is not properly convened or conducted but the decision is unanimous, the decision will be treated as binding and the irregularities overlooked.

Minutes

Section 145, CA 1963 provides that every company shall keep minutes of all general meetings at the registered office for inspection by the members of the company. Once the minutes are signed by the chairperson of the meeting, they become prima facie evidence of what happened at the meeting. Minutes of directors' meetings must also be kept, usually by the company secretary.

Section 145, CA 1963 as amended by section 19, CLEA 2001 states that a company may be ordered to produce books of minutes for the inspection of the Director of Corporate Enforcement.

Meeting of the Board of Directors

The same basic rules apply to board meetings as to general meetings. Article 101, Table A provides that directors may meet and regulate their meetings as they see fit. If board meetings need to be convened in a hurry, Article 101, Table A provides that any director may convene a meeting at any time.

The 'Indoor Management Rule'

The 'indoor management rule' or the rule in *Turquand's Case*, provides that outside third parties are entitled to presume that things done within a company were done according to correct procedures as required by the articles of association.

Royal British Bank v Turquand (1856)
The directors borrowed in excess of an authorised amount without the approval of the shareholders, and then argued that the loan from the Royal British Bank was invalid.
Held: The bank as outsiders were entitled to assume that issues of internal policy, such as the taking of votes, had been done properly. The loan was valid and had to be repaid.

The indoor management rule does not apply in cases where the facts should make the outsider enquire further, eg suspicious circumstances.

AL Underwood Ltd v Bank of Liverpool and Martins (1924)
Mr Underwood paid company cheques for AL Underwood Ltd into his personal account.
Held: The lodging of company cheques into a personal account was so unusual that the Bank should have made further enquiries and could not rely on the rule in *Turquand's Case*.

Outsiders dealing with a company are also protected by the ultra vires rule (see chapter 3).

14

MINORITY PROTECTION

Two legal provisions protect the rights of minority shareholders – the common law exceptions to the rule in *Foss v Harbottle*, and the statutory remedy of section 205, CA 1963 dealing with oppression of a minority shareholder.

The Rule in Foss v Harbottle

The rule in *Foss v Harbottle* arises out of the concept of separate legal personality.

Foss v Harbottle (1843)
Minority shareholders brought a case against company directors for misapplication of company assets.
Held: The shareholders were not the proper plaintiffs to bring such a case. Where a wrong is done to a company, the principle of separate legal personality dictates that the proper plaintiff is the company itself.

There are a number of reasons for the rule:

1. It protects the principle of separate legal personality.
2. It avoids the multiplicity of actions which would arise if individual shareholders could bring actions for wrongs done to the company.
3. If the action complained of could have been sanctioned by the company in general meeting, bringing a legal action would be futile.

O'Neil v Ryan, Ryanair Ltd and Others (1990) Ire.
The plaintiff CEO and minority shareholder sued the principal shareholder in Ryanair and the company itself, based on the reduction in value of his shares.
Held: Shareholders cannot sue for reduction in share value. This was a 'classic case to which the rule in *Foss v Harbottle* applies'.

This was followed in *Flanagan v Kelly* (1999) Ire., which held that a shareholder cannot sue a company in respect of alleged damage to his shareholding resulting from damage to the company.

Exceptions to the Rule

However, over the years, a number of exceptions have developed to the rule, allowing the minority to bring a legal action usually where the people who committed the wrong control the company. The exceptions are as follows:

1. The majority cannot sanction an act which is illegal or ultra vires the company. In such a case, the minority can always bring legal proceedings (now under section 8, CA 1963, see chapter 4).

   Parke v Daily News (1961)
   The plaintiff shareholder objected to an ultra vires gift to redundant employees.
   Held: The Court restrained the directors from paying it because it was ultra vires.

2. The majority cannot approve a wrong where proper procedures are not followed.

   Edwards v Halliwell (1950)
   An open vote was taken where rules required a secret ballot.
   Held: The minority were entitled to have the improperly taken decision set aside.

3. The majority cannot deprive a member of a personal or individual right of membership.

   Pender v Lushington (1877)
   The plaintiff's votes were rejected by the company chairperson.
   Held: The right to vote was a personal 'right of property' which the plaintiff was entitled to protect by taking a legal action against the company.

4. The majority cannot commit a wrong which would be a fraud on the minority. 'Fraud' in this context need not be dishonesty or criminal, but simply the misuse of power. Thus *Parke v Daily News* (1961) could be seen as a fraud on the minority.
   Many of the cases on breach of directors duties are also examples of fraud on the minority, such as *Cook v Deeks* in chapter 11.

5. There is also possibly a fifth exception to the rule in *Foss v Harbottle*. This was suggested by Hamilton J in *Moylan v Irish Whiting Manufacturers* (1980) Ire. In this case, the judge stated, *obiter*, that 'having regard to the provisions of Bunreacht na hEireann, I am satisfied that an exception to the rule in Foss must be made where the justice of the case demands it'.

    Balkanbank v Taher (1992), established that a 50 per cent shareholding may be a minority for the purposes of the rule in *Foss v Harbottle*, where two shareholders are deadlocked.

Form of a Shareholder's Action

A plaintiff may bring:

– a representative action on behalf of other affected shareholders
– a personal action for themselves
– a derivative action, which is an action on behalf of the company.

The Statutory Remedy for Oppression provided for in Section 205, CA 1963

Grounds for the Action under section 205

Any member of a company may apply to the court under section 205 on the grounds that 'the affairs of the company are being conducted or the powers of the directors are being exercised in a manner oppressive to a member, or in disregard of his or her interests'.

    In such circumstance the court can make such order as it sees fit, including:

– directing or prohibiting any act
– cancelling or varying any transaction
– regulating the conduct of the company's affairs in the future
– the purchase of any member's shares by other members or the company.

The court cannot make an award of compensation, except in very limited circumstances:

Irish Press plc v Ingersoll Irish Publications Ltd (1995) Ire.

Irish Press plc and Ingersoll Irish Publications Ltd created two companies to run the Irish Press newspapers, in which they held equal shares. Irish Press plc claimed oppression under section 205 when the relationship broke down and alleged that the defendants acted in their own interests rather then the interests of the Irish Press companies.

Held: Damages could not be awarded by a court under section 205, CA 1963 because that section only permitted the court to make such order as it thinks fit 'with a view to bringing to an end the matters complained of'. The award of €7.6 million in damages was made with the intention of compensating the plaintiffs rather than ending the oppression.

Because the court has such wide powers under section 205, a claim for oppression is often added on to another legal claim, such as an action for breach of director's duties.

Oppression

There is no statutory definition of oppression, but the definition of conduct which is 'burdensome, harsh or wrongful' from *Scottish Co-operative Wholesale Ltd v Mayer* (1959) has been accepted in Ireland. It is important to understand that oppressive conduct need not be illegal. The best way to understand the meaning of oppression is by looking at examples. Many of the past cases of oppression occurred in circumstances which are now covered by the Companies Acts.

Oppressive conduct need not be ongoing, but can be an isolated act.

Re Westwind Holding Co Ltd (1974) Ire.
A company sold land to the controlling shareholder–director at a very cheap price.
Held: This was oppression under section 205, CA 1963 (now covered by section 29, CA 1990, see chapter 11).

Re Williams (Tullamore) Group Ltd (1986) Ire.
Ordinary shareholders sought relief under section 205 when the company attempted to create a new category of preference shareholders, who would then obtain €169,000 in dividends which otherwise would have been distributed to the ordinary shareholders.
Held: The act proposed was oppressive as it disregarded the interests of the ordinary shareholders, and the fact that it was an isolated act was irrelevant (now covered by section 41, C(A)A 1983, see chapter 7).

Oppressive conduct is usually an ongoing series of events.

Re Greenore Trading Co Ltd (1980) Ire.
Held: Oppression occurred where a majority shareholder bought out another shareholder with a cheque drawn on the company's account, where the plaintiff was not told of this or other transactions.

Re Clubman Shirts Ltd (1983) Ire
The directors had not held AGMs or prepared accounts or reports for several years. When liquidation was likely, the directors transferred business to another company and the shareholders received no payment or information.
Held: Oppression under section 205, CA 1963
(now covered by section 150, CA 1990, see chapter 11).

Irish Press plc v Ingersoll Irish Publications Ltd (1995) Ire.
Held: There was oppression when the defendant ceased to provide management services, but insisted on the continuance of the management agreement, and that the defendant acted in their own interests and contrary to the interests of the company.

Section 205 provides that the court may permit part or all of a petition to be held in camera, ie in private, if the hearing would involve disclosure of information the publication of which would be seriously prejudicial to the interests of the company.

In *Re Irish Press Newspapers Ltd and Irish Press Publications Ltd* (1993) Ire., the Supreme Court held that there were no such danger in the Irish Press case and ordered the hearing to take place in public in the ordinary manner.

Winding Up a Company for Oppression

Section 213(f), CA 1963 provides that a company may be wound up if 'the Court is of the opinion that it would be just and equitable' to do so. This could include oppression.

Section 213(g), CA 1963 provides a company may be wound up if 'the court is satisfied that the company's affairs are being conducted, or the powers of the directors are being exercised, in a manner oppressive to any member'. Section 213(g) can be used, despite the existence of an alternative remedy; however, the court may dismiss a petition under section 213(g) if it feels proceedings under section 205 would be more appropriate.

Re Murphs Restaurants (1979) Ire.
Two of the shareholder-directors fell out with the third and removed him from the company. The third shareholder then sought to have the company wound up on the grounds that he had been treated oppressively or unfairly.
Held: It was 'just and equitable' to lift the corporate veil and wind up the company under section 213(f).

Other Statutory Protections of Minorities

Other sections in the companies acts also provide protection for minority shareholders in specific situations:

1. Dissenting shareholders in schemes of reconstruction and amalgamations are protected in sections 201–204, CA 1963 (see chapter 15).
2. Holders of 10 per cent of a company's paid up capital can requisition a meeting under section 132, CA 1963 (see chapter 13).
3. Any shareholder may require the Minister to call an AGM under section 131, CA 1963 (see chapter 13).
4. Where there is a variation of class rights, 10 per cent of the class may apply to the court to have the variation cancelled under section 38, C(A)A 1983 (see chapter 6).
5. Any shareholder may petition the court to compulsorily wind up the company on the grounds that it is 'just and equitable' to do so under section 213(f), CA 1963 (see chapter 18).
6. Any shareholder can prevent a limited company reregistering as unlimited under section 52, C(A)A 1983 (see chapter 2).
7. Shareholders may demand a poll under section 137, CA 1963 (see chapter 13).
8. The appointment of an inspector to a company can be sought by minority shareholders (see chapter 16).

15

COMPANY RE-ARRANGEMENTS

A company may re-arrange its business by transforming its capital structure, assets or ownership.

Types of Re-arrangements

1. A merger is where two or more companies combine to form united ownership, e.g. company X is wound up and its business is taken over by company Y.
2. A take-over is where company X is sold to company Y.
3. An amalgamation is where both companies X and Y are wound up, and a new company Z is created.

The Companies Acts do not classify re-arrangements under the above headings, but refer to 'arrangements and reconstructions'. In some cases, if the majority of shareholders or creditors agree to the re-arrangement, any dissenting minority will be bound by the majority decision. The Companies Acts safeguard the internal parties, and the public interest is protected by other legislation, eg competition law.

Court Sanctioned Schemes of Arrangement

Section 201, CA 1963 deals with any 'compromise or arrangement' which has the agreement of 75 per cent of the shareholders or creditors (whichever it is sought to bind). These must be sanctioned by the court. Such compromises or arrangements are rare in practice because of their complexity and the need for court approval (section 260 is more commonly used). A section 201 procedure is binding on all members.

Section 260 Reconstructions

Section 260, CA 1963 allows voluntary liquidation to be used as a means of reconstruction of companies. These are the most common type in Ireland. Section 260 allows the liquidator of a company in voluntary liquidation to sell or transfer all or part of the business to another company in exchange for shares, policies or interests in the other company. These shares, policies or interests are then distributed among members of the company which is in liquidation. Alternatively, the liquidator may arrange that instead of receiving shares, members will participate in the profits of the other company.

Company X may merge with company Y by transferring all its assets to company Y, under the section 260 procedure. The section 260 procedure may also be used where company X and company Y form company Z.

A special resolution is needed to approve such changes. Any dissenting shareholder has seven days in which to require the liquidator to stop the reconstruction or purchase the dissenter's shares. The later is the most usual outcome, and if a price cannot be agreed it will be arbitrated under the Companies Consolidation Act 1845. Thus a section 206 procedure is not binding on all members, unlike a section 201 procedure.

Take-overs

A take-over occurs where one company acquires a majority of shares in another company. This creates most problems when both are public companies. Such offers are usually conditional on a certain percentage of shareholders accepting.

Under section 204, CA 1963 the acquiring company can compulsorily acquire the shares of the dissenting minority, if 80 per cent of the shareholders in the target company have agreed.

Section 204 also allows the acquiring company to compulsorily acquire the shares of the dissenting minority if over 80 per cent agreed to transfer. The acquiring company must serve notice on the dissenters, which the court may set aside 'if it thinks fit'. The onus is on the dissenting shareholders to prove to the court that the terms of the acquisition were not fair.

If the acquiring company owns shares in the target company, it must acquire 80 per cent of the remaining shares.

Section 187, CA 1963 provides that any compensation to the directors for loss on a merger, amalgamation or take-over must be approved by the shareholders in general meeting. Any compensation not so approved will be invalid.

Control of Mergers and Take-overs

The Irish Take-over Panel Act 1997 provides for the monitoring and supervision of take-overs and some other transactions in relation to securities in certain companies. The act provides for a take-over panel and specifies principles governing the conduct of take-overs and other transactions. The act applies to Irish registered public companies whose securities are traded on the Irish Stock Exchange and other designated stock exchanges.

According to section 92, CLEA 2001, nothing in section 201–204, CA 1963 prejudices the jurisdiction of the Irish Take-over Panel Act 1997 with respect to a compromise or scheme of arrangement proposed by a company and its members.

The Competition Act 2002 contains the statutory controls for takeovers and mergers. The substantive test for vetting mergers is whether or not the result of the merger will be to 'substantially lessen competition in markets for goods and services in the State'. The Competition Authority must be notified of a merger where:

- the worldwide turnover of each of at least two of the undertakings involved is not less than €40 million, and
- the turnover in the State of at least one of the undertakings involved is not less than €40 million.

A merger which does not meet these thresholds is still subject to section 4 and section 5 of the 2002 Act. Section 4 prohibits all agreements between undertakings, decisions of associations of undertakings and concerted practices which have as their object or effect the prevention, restriction or distortion of competition in trade for any goods or services in the State. Section 5 prohibits any abuse of a dominant position in trade for any goods or services in the State.

Under the Competition Act 2002, the Minister for Enterprise Trade and Employment has ordered that all 'media mergers' be notified to the Competition Authority, irrespective of the turnover involved.

16

INVESTIGATIONS

Company Law Enforcement

The Company Law Enforcement Act 2001 established the role of the Director of Corporate Enforcement which is a corporation sole with perpetual succession. The functions of the Director under section 12, CLEA 2001 are:

- to enforce the Companies Acts, including prosecution of offences
- to encourage compliance with the Companies Acts
- to investigate suspected offences under the Companies Acts
- to refer cases of suspected indictable offences under the Companies Acts to the DPP
- to exercise a supervisory role over receivers and liquidators, where necessary and appropriate
- to ensure and enforce standards on companies and their officers in respect of the Companies Acts.

Each year the Director shall present a report to the Minister for Enterprise Trade and Employment, which the Minister shall copy to the Oireachtas.

The Director of Corporate Enforcement has the following powers, amongst others:

- to apply for restriction orders under section 150, CA 1990 (see chapter 11)
- to apply for disqualification orders under section 160, CA 1990 (see chapter 11)
- to prosecute all summary offences under the Companies Act 1963–2003
- to supervise liquidators and receivers (see chapter 18)
- to supervise companies in official and voluntary liquidation, and unliquidated insolvent companies (see chapter 18)
- to apply under section 297, CA 1963 in respect of fraudulent and reckless trading (see chapter 18)

- to freeze assets of a director under section 55, CLEA 2001 (see chapter 18)
- to initiate investigation into company affairs (see below)

The website of the Office of the Director of Corporate Enforcement is at www.odce.ie.

Investigations into Company Affairs

The Companies Act 1963 dealt with investigations into company affairs. This was replaced by Part II of the Companies Act 1990, which in turn was amended by Part III of the Company Law Enforcement Act 2001.

Court Order for Investigation

Under section 7, CA 1990 the High Court can appoint an inspector to investigate the affairs of a company. No specific circumstances are required for appointment. The following people can apply for an appointment:

- 100 shareholders or shareholders holding not less than one tenth of the paid up capital
- the company
- a creditor of the company
- in a company without a share capital, one fifth of the registered members.

The application must be supported by evidence required by the court. The costs are paid by the relevant Minister unless the court orders the costs to be paid by the applicant for the investigation or any company dealt with in the report.

Director Order for Investigation

Under section 8, CA 1990 the Director can appoint an inspector if he or she is satisfied that the circumstances suggest:

- that the company was formed for a fraudulent or improper purpose
- that the company's affairs are, or have been, conducted fraudulently, unlawfully, or in an unfairly prejudicial manner
- that persons connected with the formation or management have been guilty of fraud, misfeasance or misconduct towards the company or its shareholders

– that the members have not been given all reasonable information about a company's affairs.

Nature of an Investigation

An investigation is into 'the affairs of a company' which can be all-encompassing. It is a fact-finding operation and is not decided on issues of law. An investigation must observe fair procedures.

Inspector's Powers

An inspector may:

1. investigate a related company with the court's permission
2. compel the production of all books and documents (failure to do so may be punished as contempt of court)
3. examine under oath any person whom he or she believes to possess relevant information
4. require assistance from a company's officers and agents
5. investigate into the bank accounts of a company director where the inspector reasonably believes that money in the account is connected with misconduct, and/or if the inspector has reasonable grounds to believe that money paid in or out of the account was used for:

   – contracts in which the director had a material interest
   – loans, quasi-loans, credit transactions etc. in favour of the director or connected persons
   – exempted lending transactions by banks, which must be registered.

If an officer or agent of a company fails or refuses to produce documents, to attend before an inspector or to answer questions, the High Court may make any order it thinks fit.

Inspector's Report

The inspector must report to the High Court on completion of the investigation, and may produce interim reports. Suspicions of criminal offences may be notified to the court without an official report. The court may then make any order it sees fit.

Publication of the Report

The court must send a copy of the report to the Minister, and may order its publication and send a copy to the company. The court has discretion to omit part of the report.

A copy may be forwarded to:

- any shareholder
- any person referred to in the report
- the auditors
- the applicants for the investigation
- any person whose financial interest is affected, eg employee, creditor
- the central bank, if the report relates to a bank.

Investigation into the Ownership of Companies

Section 14, CA 1990 allows the Minister to order an inspection into who is or has been financially interested in the success or failure of a company, or able to control or influence its policy. The circumstances justifying an investigation are:

- the effective administration of company law
- the effective discharge of the Minister's function
- the public interest.

If the Minister wishes to investigate into the ownership of shares or debentures on any of the above grounds, he or she need not appoint an inspector, but simply require any person he or she believes to have the necessary information to give the names and addresses of those interested in shares and debentures, currently and previously, under section 15, CA 1990. Failure to provide such information, or the provision of false information is a criminal offence.

Inspector's Powers

The Inspector into company ownership has all the same powers as under a court inspection, except the power in relation to directors' bank accounts. The interim and final reports are the same, as is publication.

The Inspector can restrict the transfer of shares during his or her investigation. Thus there can be no share transfers, exercise of voting rights, rights issues or payment of dividends during this time. To do any of these is a criminal offence. The Minister or the court may lift these restrictions if they approve a sale of shares, or they are satisfied that all relevant information about the shares has been disclosed to the company or the Director, or that it is otherwise equitable to lift the restrictions.

Preliminary Investigations and Production of Documents

Under section 19, CA 1990 as amended by section 29, CLEA 2001, the Director has the power to carry out a preliminary search in order to decide if a formal investigation is required. The power is to access documents in a wide range of cases, and to obtain a District Court search warrant if necessary. A person who appears to be in possession of relevant information may also be searched. The Director can require the production of documents to determine whether:

– an inspector should be appointed
– the affairs of the company have been conducted with intent to defraud creditors or members
– the affairs of the company have been conducted for a fraudulent purpose
– the affairs of the company, including actual and proposed acts, have been conducted in an unfairly prejudicial manner
– the company was formed for a fraudulent or unlawful purpose.

It is a criminal offence for a person to falsify, conceal, destroy or dispose of documents when he or she knows or suspects that an investigation by a Director is being carried out.

Dunnes Stores (Ireland) Co. & Heffernan v Ryan (2002) Ire.

In a long-running challenge to the Minister's decision to appoint an authorised officer to Dunnes Stores (under the CA 1990) the Supreme Court held that an inquiry was authorised where the circumstances suggested that the affairs of the body had been conducted in a manner unfairly prejudicial to some of its members.

General Provisions

Section 14, CA 1990 was amended by section 26, CLEA 2001 to allow the court to order, on the application of the Director, that a company subject to an investigation shall be liable to repay the investigation expenses to the Director. Other people may also be ordered to repay some or all of the director's expenses – a person convicted as a result of an investigation, a person ordered to pay damages as a result of an investigation and a person awarded damages as a result of an investigation.

The Inspector's report is admissible in civil legal proceedings as evidence of the Inspector's opinion.

The Inspector's powers extend to foreign companies which carry on or have carried on business in Ireland. The Director may exercise his or her power to assist overseas company law authorities.

17

EXAMINERSHIPS

The Companies (Amendment) Act 1990 introduced the concept of the examiner in company law. The Act was introduced against the background of the possible liquidation of the Goodman Group, and consequently is known as the 'Goodman Act'.

The aim of the legislation is to prevent companies being put into receivership or wound up, by putting them under court protection for 70 days.

The rushed introduction of the C(A)A 1990 led to it containing flaws which were considered by the Company Law Review Group in its 1994 report. The recommendations made by the group were enacted into Part II of the Companies (Amendment) (No. 2) Act 1999 which amends the C(A)A 1990. The major changes are that the application to appoint an examiner must be accompanied by a report of an independent accountant, and an examiner will only be appointed if a company has a 'reasonable prospect of survival'. The protection for creditors, particularly secured creditors, is also improved.

Appointment

The ground for appointment is that a company is unable to pay its debts, or is unlikely to be able to pay its debts as they fall due. The tests are whether the company can pay its debts as they fall due, or whether its assets are less than liabilities, or if a debt of €1,270 is outstanding. Usually the appointment order is made to facilitate the survival of the company as a going concern. The company must not already be in liquidation.

However, the High Court shall not appoint an examiner unless it is satisfied that there is a reasonable prospect of the survival of the whole or part of the company as a going concern. (This replaced the C(A)A 1990 standard of 'some' prospect of survival.) as stated by the Supreme Court in *Re Atlantic Magnets Ltd (in receivership)* (1993) Ire.

An application can be made by:

- the company
- the directors

- a creditor, or contingent or prospective creditor, including an employee
- a member with at least 10 per cent of the votes.

In the case of an insurance company or bank, the application can only be made by the Minister for Enterprise, Trade and Employment or the Central Bank. The onus is on the party making the application to prove the company's reasonable prospect of survival, according to *Re Tuskar Resources plc* (2001) Ire.

On hearing the application, the High Court has discretion to appoint an examiner, refuse, adjourn the petition, make an interim order or make such order as it thinks fit. An examiner may also be appointed to a related company.

Powers and Duties

Like a liquidator, an examiner is not required to have any professional qualification, but is usually an accountant. An examiner receives pay and expenses in a similar way to a liquidator, ie determined by the court. The examiner has powers similar to an auditor in relation to accessing information and convening meetings. The examiner can apply to the High Court for directions on any question. The examiner may take over management powers in exceptional cases.

The examiner's duty is to conduct 'an examination of the affairs of a company' and report to the court within twenty-one days. At this point the examiner must report on whether he thinks the company can survive as a going concern, and what steps should be taken to ensure this. The examiner may take over the director's management powers if the court thinks it is just and equitable to do so.

Independent Accountant's Report

Critics of the C(A)A 1990 believed that it was too easy to appoint an examiner and that in many cases it merely postponed the inevitable liquidation. Under section 7, C(A)(No. 2)A 1999 a report by an independent accountant will accompany the petition for examinership. This accountant should either be the auditor of the company, or someone qualified to be its examiner. According to *Re Tuskar Resources plc* (2001) Ire., the independent accountant may be appointed examiner (although this may be undesirable in some cases).

The report shall contain a statement of affairs of the company detailing its assets and liabilities (including contingent and prospective liabilities), and listing creditors and their securities.

The accountant's report will also state his or her opinion on whether the company or any part of it has a reasonable prospect of survival as a going concern, and whether formulation and acceptance of a compromise or scheme of arrangement would offer a reasonable prospect of survival. A draft compromise or scheme of arrangement may be included.

The accountant's report must detail the funding required to enable the company to continue trading during examinership, and the source of such funding. It also should detail his or her recommendations on which liabilities incurred before the presentation of the petition should be paid, and whether a creditors' committee is appropriate. The accountant may also include such other matters as he or she thinks relevant. (The accountant may express a view on proceedings under section 297, CA 1963 re fraudulent or reckless trading (see chapter 18).)

In exceptional cases, if the report of the independent accountant is not available in time to accompany the petition, the court may place a company under interim protection pending the report for a period of up to ten days. The prior appointment of a receiver to the company is not exceptional circumstances. If the report is not available at the end of the extended time, the company shall cease to be under court protection. The directors of a company must co-operate with the independent accountant.

Petition to Appoint an Examiner

Under section 10, C(A)(No. 2)A 1999 creditors now have the right to be heard during the court hearing to consider appointment of an examiner. Each creditor who indicates his or her desire to be heard by the court in an application to appoint an examiner shall be given an opportunity. A creditor may also apply in writing to the independent accountant for a copy of his or her report.

Under section 13, C(A)(No. 2)A 1999 the petitioner and the independent accountant have a duty to disclose any information which is material to the exercise of the court's powers, and must act in good faith. Failure to do so will result in the court declining to hear the petition. (In effect, this applied before 1999, as a result of *Re Wogans (Drogheda) Ltd* (No. 2) (1992) Ire., where the judge was very critical of a company director who had not disclosed large sums owing to the Revenue during the petition to appoint an examiner.)

Section 21 C(A)(No. 2)A 1999 provides that the court may hold a hearing to consider evidence of substantial disappearance of company property which is not adequately accounted for, or other serious irregularities.

Effect of the Examiner's Appointment

1. No winding up or receivership can commence.
2. A receivership created within the last three days ceases to operate.
3. No legal actions can be initiated against the company, except with the consent of the examiner.
4. No recovery of goods under retention of title clauses or hire purchase can take place.
5. The examiner may take over the director's management powers if the court thinks it is just and equitable to do so.

Course of an Examinership

An examinership lasts for seventy days under the 1999 Act. The appointment of an examiner must be advertised in *Iris Oifigiúil* and two daily papers, and the company must amend all its documentation to include 'in Examination' after the company name.

Under the C(A)(No. 2) Act 1999 an examiner's ability to repudiate contracts is now confined to contracts entered into during the period of examinership only (with the exception of negative pledges which can be set aside if the examiner believes that their enforcement would prejudice the survival of the company).

As soon as practicable after an examiner is appointed, he or she must formulate proposals for a compromise or scheme of arrangement. This will form the basis of the examiner's final report to the court. The examiner must formulate such proposals, hold meetings of creditors and members and report to court on proposals within thirty-five days of being appointed. Meetings of members are for information only.

This report states the opinion that the company is capable of survival as a going concern, the necessary conditions, and recommendations of what course of action is to be taken including a compromise or scheme of arrangement. The examiner must formulate proposals for such a scheme if it is recommended. These must be accepted by a majority of the different classes which will be affected by the proposals.

The examiner's report must be considered by the High Court. The court will approve the proposals if:

– they are accepted by one class of members and creditors whose interests are impaired by the implementation of the proposals
– they are fair and equitable to classes who have not accepted it and whose interests would be impaired, and
– they are not primarily for tax avoidance purposes.

Once approved, the proposals will be binding on everyone concerned. If the examiner is unable to formulate proposals for compromise, he or she may apply to the court for directions. The court may make such order as it sees fit, including winding up the company if it is just and equitable to do so.

Any member or creditor whose interests would be impaired by implementation of the proposals can object to the court on a number of specified grounds, but not if he or she voted for acceptance of the proposal. In *Re Casteholding Investment Co. Ltd* (2001) Ire., the court held that a creditor bank was not being unfairly prejudiced, as all creditors were being treated equally. The court also stated that it can modify a scheme but not rewrite it.

When a company is in examinership, the court has power to make company officers liable for fraudulent and reckless trading (the same as in liquidation, see chapter 18).

Companies which have undergone the examinership process and are still trading include the Goodman Group and Xtravision. Companies which went into liquidation following examinership include United Meat Packers and Don Bluth Studios.

In the case of *Re Holidair* (1994) the Supreme Court decided the following points:

- An examiner can be appointed after the appointment of a receiver. (The act provides that an examiner can be appointed within three days of a receiver, but this had not previously been tested in the Courts.)
- A floating charge which crystallised on the appointment of a receiver became a floating charge once again on the appointment of an examiner.
- A charge over book debts which was described as fixed was in fact a floating charge because the class of assets changed from time to time, and there was no restriction on the companies drawing monies from these accounts.
- The examiner can borrow without the consent of the secured creditors. This has been much criticised by creditors and financial institutions.

Priority of Costs in an Examinership

A criticism of the 1990 Act, as highlighted in *Re Holidair*, was the examiner's ability to secure new company borrowings ahead of the existing secured creditors. Section 28, C(A)(No. 2)A 1999 now provides that the pay, costs and expenses of an examiner which have been sanctioned by the court, shall be paid in full before any other claim secured or unsecured in any receivership or liquidation. Liabilities incurred by the company to which an examiner has been appointed are treated as expenses of the examiner and shall be paid before any other claim including a floating charge, but after a mortgage, charge, lien or encumbrance of a fixed charge, in any receivership or liquidation.

In effect, the order of priorities in an examinership is now:

1. examiner's fees and expenses
2. fixed charges
3. liabilities certified by examiner, eg borrowing
4. preferential debts
5. floating charges.

18

LIQUIDATIONS

Types of Liquidations

A liquidation is the dissolution of a company. A liquidator will sell all the company's assets and pay the company's debts in order of priority.

There are two categories of liquidations:

1. compulsory liquidation (also known as court liquidation)
2. voluntary liquidation, which can be either: (a) a member's voluntary winding up, or (b) a creditor's voluntary winding up

Compulsory Liquidation

A compulsory liquidation is the least common type of liquidation, where the decision to wind up is forced upon the company, and ordered by the High Court.

Grounds for Compulsory Liquidation

There are three main grounds for seeking a liquidation:

1. A company is unable to pay its debts (the most commonly used ground). 'Unable to pay its debts' may be decided according to the balance sheet test, ie where assets are less than liabilities, or where a company is unable to pay its debts as they fall due. An unpaid debt of €1,270 or more can also lead to liquidation.
2. A company's affairs are being managed in an oppressive way under section 205, CA 1963. (See chapter 14.)

   Re Murph's Restaurant Ltd (1979) Ire.
   Two shareholder-directors removed the third from the company after their personal relationships soured. In response, the third man sought to wind up the company on the grounds of oppression under section 205, CA 1963.
   Held: It was just and equitable to lift the corporate veil and wind up the company, because the removal of the third man damaged a

relationship based on 'mutual trust and confidence' which was more akin to a partnership than a company.

3. Where it is just and equitable to do so.

Re Murph's Restaurant Ltd is also an example of this category, but the two grounds are not the same.

Re German Date Coffee Co (1882)
A company was formed with the object of making coffee from dates. When it failed to get a patent, it began to make coffee from coffee beans. A shareholder objected to the change of business and sought to wind up the company.
Held: It was just and equitable to liquidate the company because it had exceeded its powers.

4. Other grounds for compulsory liquidation:

   - the company has resolved by special resolution that it may be wound up by the court
   - the company did not commence business within one year of incorporation, or suspended business for a whole year
   - that the number of members is reduced below seven in a plc.

Seeking a Compulsory Liquidation
The petition to compulsorily liquidate a company may be entered in the High Court by:

- a creditor or creditors
- the company itself
- the Minister for Enterprise, Trade and Employment
- any shareholder under section 205, CA 1963
- any contributory, i.e. person liable to contribute to company if wound up.

The procedure is that a petition is made in the High Court. If the High Court makes an appointment, the winding up order is back-dated to the date of the petition. A statement of affairs must be filed in the High Court within twenty-one days. The court may appoint a Committee of Inspection (made up of creditors) to help the liquidator.

Re Dunleckney Ltd (1999) Ire.
Held: Failure to make a statutory statement of affairs was sufficient reason to restrict the director under section 150, CA 1990 (see chapter 11.)

Voluntary Liquidation

All voluntary liquidations begin with a resolution of a general meeting to liquidate the company.

A Members' Voluntary Liquidation

A members' voluntary liquidation occurs when the company's members decide to wind up the company while solvent, eg the shareholders decide to divide the money and retire. A member's voluntary liquidation begins with a declaration of solvency, stating that the company will be able to pay all its debts within twelve months. This declaration is made by the directors and an accountant, and as a result, the company's creditors take no part in the winding up, ie there is no committee of inspection as they trust the company to pay the debts.

When the liquidator is appointed, their appointment is not back-dated. In a member's voluntary liquidation there will usually be a surplus left after all the debts have been paid which will be distributed among the shareholders.

A Creditors' Voluntary Liquidation

A creditors' voluntary liquidation occurs when the creditors of a company seek to liquidate it, with the assistance of the company. In this case there is no declaration of solvency. There will be a creditors' meeting and a committee of inspection appointed to help the liquidator. A creditors' voluntary liquidation is used where the creditors believe that the company is unable to pay its debts as an alternative to compulsory liquidation. The creditors choose the liquidator, or leave it to the company. A creditor's nominee as liquidator is chosen by a majority in value only of creditors present personally or by proxy voting in favour.

A members' voluntary liquidation may be converted into a creditors' voluntary liquidation if the liquidator does not believe that the declaration of solvency is true. A director who made a false declaration of solvency may be made personally liable without limit for the debts of the company.

Role of the Director of Corporate Enforcement in
Voluntary Liquidations

Section 49, Company Law Enforcement Act 2001 inserted a new section into the section 282, CA 1963 Act which gives the court the power to order the Director of Corporate Enforcement to inspect the books of a company in voluntary liquidation. Officers must facilitate the Director. At the Director's request or on its own devices, the court may examine any person known or suspected to:

- have possession of company property, or
- who is indebted to the company, or
- who is capable of giving information about the promotion, formation, trade, dealings, affairs or property of the company.

Failure to attend examination is contempt of court and may lead to the arrest of the person to be examined.

The court may order a person indebted to the company to pay the debt to the liquidator, and order a person who possesses company documents and property to convey these to the liquidator. The court also has power to allow the Director or liquidator to enter and search the premises of such a person. Obstruction is a criminal offence. The court has the power to arrest an absconding officer or contributory.

Liquidator's Activities

Once appointed, the liquidator must notify the Registrar of Companies, who in turn will notify the Director of Corporate Enforcement.

Regardless of the type of liquidation, a liquidator's duties are the same. The duties are fiduciary. The liquidator must sell the assets, pay the debts and distribute any surplus. He or she must pay:

- the costs of the liquidation
- the fixed charges in the order in which they were created
- the preferential debts (*pari passu* or equally)
- the floating charges in the order in which they were created
- the unsecured creditors
- any return to the shareholders.

Preferential debts in section 285, CA 1963 are:

- all local rates within the last twelve months
- all assessed taxes not exceeding one year's assessment
- all PRSI in the last year

– all wages or salary within the last four months
– all accrued holiday pay.

Disclaim Unprofitable Contracts

The liquidator may disclaim unprofitable contracts under section 290, CA 1963, with the permission of the High Court. The court may require notice of the disclaimer to be given to any person interested and impose such conditions as it thinks just.

Fraudulent Preference

Any charge or transaction may be invalid under section 286, CA 1963 as a fraudulent preference, if it was created within six months of a winding up. Section 286 prohibits 'any conveyance, mortgage, delivery of goods, payment, execution, or other act relating to property' done by an insolvent company which has the effect of preferring one creditor over another in the event of a liquidation. Such fraudulent preferences are invalid.

The burden of proof is on the liquidator, but a transaction or preference is presumed to be fraudulent and the six-month period is extended to two years, if it is in favour of a director or a connected person. A connected person is a director, a shadow director, a director's spouse, parent, brother, sister or child, a partner of a director or the trustee of a trust which benefits a director, their spouse, child or a company which the director controls.

Payments made in the normal course of dealings, or in response to pressure, are not fraudulent preferences.

Re K M Kushler Ltd (1943)
Held: The liquidator must prove an intention to prefer at the time the transaction was made. An inference may be drawn from the facts if no other explanation is open to the liquidator.

Station Motors Ltd v AIB (1985) Ire.
A company's overdraft with AIB was personally guaranteed by two directors. Three months later the company went into creditors' voluntary liquidation. Prior to the liquidation, almost half of the overdraft had been repaid. The liquidator argued that these payments were a fraudulent preference.
Held: The pre-liquidation repayment of the overdraft was done to prefer AIB directly and the guarantors indirectly. This transaction was set aside by the liquidator and AIB had to repay the money to the company.

Business Communications Ltd v Baxter and Parsons (1995) Ire.
Prior to the company going to insolvent liquidation, €38,000 was
paid to AIB to reduce the company's overdraft, and thereby reduce
the directors' personal liability as guarantors.
Held: This was a fraudulent preference.

Avoidance of Floating Charges

A liquidator may avoid a floating charge under section 288, CA 1963
if it was registered within twelve months of a liquidation and the
company was not solvent at its creation. A floating charge created
within two years of an insolvent liquidation may be invalid if the
charge was in favour of a director or a connected person.

However, if money was advanced to a company by a creditor when
the floating charge was created, section 288 does not apply as the
company is deemed to be solvent. In other words, if a creditor
advances fresh funds to the company when the floating charge is
created, it is solvent at that time.

Re Daniel Murphy Ltd (1964) Ire.
A company borrowed €19,000 from their bank in return for a floating charge. Two weeks after the delayed registration of the charge,
the company went into liquidation. Between the creation of the
floating charge and the liquidation, the company had lodged cheques
for €38,000 in its bank account, and debited a similar amount.
Held: The bank lent money to the company at the time of creation of
the floating charge, thus the company was solvent at that time due to
a fresh advance of funds.

Fraudulent Trading

Section 297, CA 1963 as amended by section 138, 1990 CA states
'any person knowingly a party to carrying on the business of a
company with intent to defraud creditors of the company or for any
fraudulent purpose shall be guilty of an offence'. Fraudulent trading
is usually prosecuted when a company is in liquidation (although this
is not a condition.) A person found guilty of fraudulent trading may
be fined and/or imprisoned and made personally liable without limit
for the debts of the company.

Any persons knowingly involved can be convicted of fraudulent
trading, even though that person may have no connection on paper
with the company.

Re Kelly's Carpetdrome Ltd (1983) Ire.

A supermarket ceased trading and its stock was taken over by Kelly's Carpetdrome, which had the same directors. All the supermarket's creditors were paid prior to it being liquidated except the Revenue Commissioners. Money was transferred from Carpetdrome to other companies controlled by the directors. When it became apparent that the Revenue Commissioners were about to seek monies owed to them, the stock of Carpetdrome was transferred to another company controlled by the same men, Kelly's Carpet Drive-In Ltd, and all Carpetdrome's debts were paid except the Revenue Commissioners. Carpetdrome Ltd went into liquidation owing large sums to the Revenue Commissioners. The liquidator discovered falsification and destruction of records within the company.

Held: The directors had acted deliberately to defraud the Revenue Commissioners and were made personally liable for the debts of Carpetdrome.

Re Aluminium Fabricators Ltd (1983) Ire.

Directors of a company siphoned off the assets for their own benefit and maintained two sets of accounts to conceal their actions from their auditors, creditors and the Revenue Commissioners. Company money had been used to buy cars and an aeroplane for the directors.

Held: The directors' actions constituted fraudulent trading and they were made personally liable without limit for all the debts of the company.

Re Synnott (1996) Ire.

Mark Synnott (Life and Pensions) Brokers Ltd traded insolvently for fourteen years before the company went into insolvent liquidation with debts of €2.5 million. Synnott, one of the directors, was charged with fraudulent trading of €50,000, which he allegedly solicited as investments from customers when he knew the company was insolvent.

Held: This was fraudulent trading, and the first conviction under the CA 1990.

Normally fraudulent trading is a continuous pattern, but a once-off transaction can also be fraudulent trading.

Re Hunting Lodges Ltd (1985) Ire.

A company's main asset was a pub 'Durty Nelly's' which was valued at €950,000. The company was insolvent and had debts to the Revenue Commissioners. The pub was sold for €610,000 and an additional €254,000 was paid in a secret transaction.

Held: An isolated transaction could, and did, constitute fraudulent trading in this case, and was done with intention to defraud creditors, ie the Revenue.

Reckless Trading

Reckless trading lacks the intent of fraudulent trading, ie reckless trading is more like negligence or carelessness. Section 297, CA 1963 as amended by section 138, CA 1990 creates personal liability without limit for officers carrying on business in a reckless manner or when they ought to know it would cause loss to a company's creditors. The concept of reckless trading was introduced in 1990 to cover situations when intention of fraud cannot be proven. However, it is still difficult to prove.

Re Hefferon Kearns Ltd (No. 1) (1993) Ire.
Held: The reckless trading provisions did not have retrospective effect and directors could only be liable for trading which occurred after the coming into force of the 1990 Act.

Re Hefferon Kearns Ltd (No. 2) (1993)
The defendants were directors in a building company and held 85 per cent of the shares. The company was involved in three major contracts, two of which were for companies in which the directors also held shares. The company got into financial difficulties and an examiner was appointed. The examiner sought to make the directors personally liable for the company's debts due to reckless trading. It was argued that the director's behaviour leading to the examinership was reckless. The High Court held that the directors had not traded recklessly, for the reasons outlined below.

The following important points of law were laid down:

- It is not necessary to prove fraud in an action for reckless trading.
- The reckless trading legislation does not impose collective responsibility on the board of directors; thus the case has to be proven against each separate director based on their conduct.
- For a director to be 'knowingly' involved in reckless trading, he must have been a party to carrying on business in a manner which he knew very well involved a serious and obvious risk of loss or damage to others, and ignored that risk, because he did not care whether such others suffered loss or damage, or because his own selfish desire overrode any concern which he ought to have had for others.

– Thus, the law requires knowledge or imputed knowledge that a director's actions *would* cause loss to creditors; so that worry or uncertainty about the company's ability to pay was not sufficient to create liability.

Held: To prove reckless trading, the directors must know of an obvious and serious risk of loss or damage to others, and ignore this risk, or be careless and indifferent to the consequences. Worry or uncertainty is not the same as knowledge.

Misfeasance Proceeding

Misfeasance under section 298, CA 1963 is an action for recovery of money misapplied by an officer of a company. This action has largely been superseded by the newer provisions on fraudulent and reckless trading. Officers and members of a company can also be prosecuted for other criminal offences.

The Director of Corporate Enforcement

The Company Law Enforcement Act 2001 gives a role to the Director of Corporate Enforcement in liquidations. Section 56 provides that within six months of appointment, the liquidator of an insolvent company must report to the Director on the conduct of the company directors. Section 56 also provides that a liquidator of an insolvent company shall subsequently apply to the court to restrict the directors under section 150, CA 1990 (see chapter 11).

Section 57 gives the Director power to examine the liquidator's books. A member, creditor or contributory may request the Director to do so, or the Director may act alone. The Director can examine the books of an individual liquidation or all those carried out by the liquidator. Section 58 provides that if a professional body disciplinary committee makes a finding of misconduct by a member during a receivership or liquidation, the body shall report the matter to the Director.

Under section 243, CA 1963 as amended by section 43, CLEA 2001, the court may order the inspection of company documents by the Director, as well as creditors and contributors.

The liquidator or Director may get a court order to enter the dwelling of a person indebted to the company or possessing company documents, to search and seize company documents, property or money found on the premises. Obstruction of such a search is a criminal offence.

As explained in chapter 11, under section 55, CLEA 2001 the Director or others, may seek a court order to prohibit a director or officer from removing his or her assets from the State or to reduce his or her assets within or outside the State below a specified amount, in certain circumstances.

19

PARTNERSHIP LAW

Section 1 of the Partnership Act 1890 defines a partnership as 'a relationship which subsists between persons carrying on a business in common with a view to profit'. A business includes any 'trade, occupation or profession' according to section 45. The 1890 Act remains the main piece of legislation regulating partnerships.

There must be at least two partners, and a maximum of twenty, according to the CA 1963. Since the C(A)A 1983, a partnership of accountants or solicitors may have in excess of twenty members.

If a partnership is carried on under a name other than the surnames of all members, that name must be registered under the Registration of Business Names Act 1963.

Formation of Partnership

Unlike companies, there are no set formalities for creating a partnership; an express or implied agreement of the parties is sufficient. The parties may create a partnership agreement, but this is not compulsory.

Partnership Agreement

A partnership agreement or 'articles of partnership' is a written deed which will usually cover the following issues:

– the names of the partners
– the name of the firm and its location
– the date of formation of the partnership and its duration
– the nature of the business
– the capital of the firm and the amount contributed by each partner
– the ratio in which profits and losses are to be shared
– the keeping of regular accounts and preparation of annual accounts
– the drawings each partner can make from the business
– the firm's auditors
– the assets of the partnership
– the powers and duties of partners

- the procedure for arbitrating on disputes
- the admission and expulsion of partners
- the effect of death, retirement or bankruptcy of a partner
- the calculating of goodwill on death or retirement of a partner
- the dissolution of the partnership.

The parties are free to include such other terms as they wish. Section 19, PA 1890 provides that the rights and duties of the partners may be varied on the consent of all.

Relationship of Partners to Third Parties

The relationships of partners to third parties deals with the issue of partners acting as agents. Under section 5, PA 1890, 'every partner is an agent of the firm and the other partners for the purpose of the business of the partnership'. This is the actual authority of a partner as agent. The acts of such a partner bind the firm and other partners.

A partner may still bind the firm through apparent (or ostensible) authority, unless the third party with whom a partner deals is aware that a partner lacks authority to contract.

The limits on section 5 are that the act:

- must be related to the business of the firm
- must be done in the name of the partnership (and not the partner)
- must be usual for a partner to do in carrying on the business.

Partners have been held to have actual authority to buy and sell goods, hire and fire staff, write and accept cheques, borrow money and give security. Partners do not have actual authority to execute a deed, pledge the firm's goods as security or submit a dispute to arbitration.

A firm may limit the actual authority of a partner, eg to transactions under €500. However, as third parties may not be aware of this limit, transactions in excess of the limit may be valid under apparent authority, and enforceable by the third party.

Relationship of Partners with Each Other

Section 9, PA 1890 states that each partner is jointly liable for the debts of the firm incurred while he or she was a partner. Liability will end when the partner's appointment ends.

However, unless third parties are notified that X is no longer a partner, X will retain apparent authority. There are two consequences of this:

- X will be bound by any debts on contracts made by the firm after his or her retirement
- X can bind the firm if he or she makes a contract in the firm's name of the type that the firm would be able to make.

Thus it is in the interest of both the retiring partner and the firm to publicise the fact of the retirement and so end the apparent authority. This must be done by an advertisement in *Iris Oifigiúil*, and in any applicable trade journal. All creditors of the firm should be personally informed, and the retiring partner's name should be removed from all stationery and documents.

Partners' Duties

Partners owe fiduciary duties to each other. Other duties are usually provided for in the partnership agreement. These duties may be varied on the consent of all, under section 19, PA 1890.

Section 24(1), PA 1890 provides that all partners share equally in the profits of the company and must contribute equally towards the losses.

Section 24(2), PA 1890 provides that the firm must indemnify partners in respect of payments made and personal liabilities incurred in the ordinary conduct of the business, or in respect of necessary things done to preserve the business or partnership.

Section 28, PA 1890 provides that partners must give each other true accounts and full information of all things relating to the partnership.

Common law provides that every partner must account to the firm for any personal profit or benefit obtained without the consent of the other partners' from any transaction relating to the partnership, its name, property or business connections.

Management

Section 24, PA 1890 provides that every partner is entitled to take part in the management of the business, but is not entitled to payment for so doing.

Section 24(6), PA 1890 provides that no new partner may be introduced without the unanimous consent of existing partners.

Section 24(8), PA 1890 provides that any dispute about the business may be decided by a majority of the partners. However, a change in the nature of the business requires unanimous consent.

Section 24(9), PA 1890 provides that every partner has the right to access, inspect and get a copy of the partnership books.

Changing Partners

Section 24(6), PA 1890 provides that no new partners may be introduced without the unanimous consent of existing partners.

Section 25, PA 1890 provides that a partner cannot be expelled by a majority decision unless there is an express power of expulsion in the partnership agreement which has been exercised in good faith.

A new partner will be jointly liable for debts incurred by the partnership from the date of their appointment, but not prior, unless they specifically agree to be so bound.

Ending of Partnership

A partnership can end in three ways:

- by agreement of the parties
- by operation of law
- by order of the court.

Section 19, PA 1890 provides that a partnership may be dissolved at any time by the consent of all parties.

Section 32–34, PA 1890 provides that, subject to agreement to the contrary, a partnership is dissolved by operation of law:

- upon the expiry of a fixed term
- upon the completion of a single venture
- upon one party giving notice to another, if it is a partnership at will
- upon the death or bankruptcy of a partner (unless the contrary is provided for in the partnership agreement)
- where the partnership agreement would become frustrated.

Section 32–35, PA 1890 permits a partner to apply to court to dissolve a partnership. The court may dissolve a partnership:

- if a partner becomes insane
- if a partner becomes permanently incapacitated
- if a partner has been found guilty of any conduct which is seriously damaging to the business of the firm
- if a partner wilfully and persistently breaks the partnership agreement
- if the partnership can only be carried on at a loss
- if it is just and equitable in the circumstances.

Section 37, PA 1890 provides that a partner can notify the public of the dissolution.

On dissolution, section 39 provides that the partnership property is applied to pay the firm's debts and liabilities, and any surplus is returned to the partners.

Partnerships versus Companies

The difference between a partnership and a company are as follows:

1. Name

A partnership will be called something like 'Murphy and Partners' or 'Murphy and Company'. A partnership cannot use the word 'limited' in its name.

A company must use the word 'limited' in its name, such as Murphy & Co Ltd or Murphy plc.

2. Size

A partnership can have between two and twenty partners, ie members, except in the case of accountants and solicitors, who can have up to fifty partners.

A private company can have between one and fifty shareholders.

A public company can have seven or more shareholders.

3. Separate Legal Personality

A partnership has no separate legal personality from its members.

A company has a legal personality distinct and separate from its shareholders. A company can own property in its own name, employ people, have its own bank accounts etc.

4. Limited Liability

A partnership has unlimited liability, ie all the partners are liable without limit for the debts of the firm. However, there may be partners who have limited liability under the Limited Partnerships Act 1907, provided at least one partner has unlimited liability.

A company has limited liability, ie the debts of a shareholder are limited to any amounts they owe on their shares. In practice, this is seen as the greatest advantage of a company.

5. Succession

When one partner dies, the partnership is dissolved (unless the partnership agreement provides otherwise).

A company has 'Perpetual Succession', that is it lasts forever, or until it is wound up. If one or all of the shareholders dies, the company continues with new members.

6. Management

A partnership is governed by the partners acting together.

A company is managed by directors on behalf of the shareholders.

7. Shares

A partnership does not have legal 'shares' and a partner's interest cannot be transferred to another person without the consent of the other partners.

A company has shares which are said to be freely transferable, although in practice shares in a private company are subject to restrictions on transfer.

8. Regulation

A partnership may create a Partnership Agreement to regulate its functioning.

A company must have a memorandum of association and articles of association to regulate it.

9. Legislation

A partnership is governed by the Partnerships Act 1890, and the Limited Partnership Act 1907.

A company is governed by the Companies Acts 1963–2003.

Limited Partnership

Generally, the liability of partners is unlimited. However, a limited partnership can be created under the Limited Partnerships Act 1907. A limited partnership is one where there is at least one general partner with unlimited liability for the firm's debts, and at least one limited partner with liability limited to their initial contribution to the firm.

A limited partner cannot take part in the company's management. The death, bankruptcy or insanity of a limited partner does not dissolve a partnership.

A limited partnership must be registered with the Registrar of Companies. Very few limited partnerships have been formed since the Companies Act 1963 introduced the concept of limited liability for companies.

The Investment Limited Partnerships Act 1994 allows for the creation of specialised limited partnerships to operate in the International Financial Services Centre.

INDEX